C000252338

art

Baedeker's

STUTTGART

Imprint

Cover picture: The Stiftskirche, with the Old Palace and the Mercury Column

96 colour photographs
17 ground-plans, 8 special plans, 4 graphic representations, 1 transport plan (trams and S-Bahn), 1 city plan

Conception: Redaktionsbüro Harenberg, Schwerte

Text: Helmut Linde

Editorial work: Baedeker Stuttgart
English Language: Alec Court

General direction:
Dr Peter Baumgarten, Baedeker Stuttgart

Cartography:
Georg Schiffner & Christoph Gallus, Lahr
Mairs Geographischer Verlag GmbH & Co., Ostfildern-Kemnat (city plan)

English translation: James Hogarth

Source of illustrations:
Allianz (1), Baumgarten (2), Daimler-Benz AG (2), Deutsches Landwirtschaftsmuseum (1), Didoni (1), Elsasser (1), Historia-Photo (6), Landesbildstelle Württemberg (5), Lang (1), Nahm (57), Planck (1), Rudel (1), Staatsgalerie (2), Stadtplanungsamt (6), Verkehrsamt (6), Württembergisches Landesmuseum (3).

Following the tradition established by Karl Baedeker in 1844, sights of particular interest and hotels and restaurants of particular quality are distinguished by either one or two asterisks.

To make it easier to locate the various sights listed in the "A to Z" section of the Guide, their coordinates on the large city plan (and on the smaller inset plan of the city centre) are shown in red at the head of each entry.

Only a selection of hotels, restaurants and shops can be given: no reflection is implied, therefore, on establishments not included.

In a time of rapid change it is difficult to ensure that all the information given is entirely accurate and up to date, and the possibility of error can never be completely eliminated. Although the publishers can accept no responsibility for inaccuracies and omissions, they are always grateful for corrections and suggestions for improvement.

© Baedeker Stuttgart
Original German edition

© 1987 Jarrold and Sons Ltd
English language edition world-wide

© 1987 The Automobile Association 57228
United Kingdom and Ireland

US and Canadian Edition
Prentice Hall Press

Licensed user:
Mairs Geographischer Verlag GmbH & Co., Ostfildern-Kemnat bei Stuttgart

Reproductions: Gölz Repro-Service GmbH, Ludwigsburg

The name *Baedeker* is a registered trademark

Printed in Great Britain by Jarrold Printing, Norwich

0-13-058223-9 US & Canada
0 86145 410-3 UK
3-87504-114-3 Germany

Contents

Useful Telephone Numbers

Emergencies
  Police, accident   110

Emergencies	
Police, accident	110
Fire	112
First aid, rescue service	28 02 11
Medical emergency service (Ärztlicher Notdienst)	28 02 11
Chemists – 24-hour service	22 43 10
Breakdown assistance	
ACE	53 44 44
ADAC	1 92 11
AvD	77 55 18
DKSV	60 54 01

Information	
Tourist Office	2 22 80
Flight information	7 90 13 88
Train information	29 97 11

Aid for disabled	68 20 41

Airlines	
British Airways	29 94 71
Lufthansa	2 04 41
PanAm	79 90 01
TWA	61 05 81

Consulates	
United Kingdom	22 03 59
USA	24 25 65

Lost property	
Municipal Lost Property Office	2 16–20 16
Railways	20 92–54 68
Tramways	7 88 50
Post Office	2 06 71

Motoring organisations	
ADAC	28 00–1 11
ACE	50 67–1

Taxis	56 60 61

Telephone	
Services	11 41
Directory inquiries, inland	11 88
Directory inquiries, international	0 01 18
International exchange	00 10
Dialling code, United Kingdom	00 44
Dialling code, United States or Canada	00 1

Telegrams	11 31

Preface

This Pocket Guide to Stuttgart is one of the new generation of Baedeker guides.

Baedeker pocket guides, illustrated throughout in colour, are designed to meet the needs of the modern traveller. They are quick and easy to consult, with the principal features of interest described in alphabetical order and practical details about location, opening times, etc., shown in the margin.

Each city guide is divided into three parts. The first part gives a general account of the city, its history, notable personalities and so on; in the second part its principal sights are described; and the third part contains a variety of practical information designed to help visitors to find their way about and make the most of their stay.

The Baedeker pocket guides are noted for their concentration on essentials and their convenience of use. They contain numerous specially drawn plans and coloured illustrations. At the back of the book is a large plan of the city. Each entry in the main part of the guide gives the coordinates of the square on the plan in which the particular feature can be located. Users of this guide, therefore, will have no difficulty in finding what they want to see.

Facts and Figures

Stuttgart's
coat of arms

General

Stuttgart, described as a "city amid forests and vineyards", is the third largest conurbation in the Federal Republic of Germany, capital of the *Land* of Baden-Württemberg and chief town of the administrative region (*Regierungsbezirk*) that bears its name.

Stuttgart lies in latitude 48° 46′ 36″ N and longitude 9° 10′ 48″ E. The highest point within the city area is the Bernhartshöhe (549 m (1,801 ft)), just north of the Stuttgart–Vaihingen motorway intersection; the lowest point is the River Neckar in the Hofen district (207 m (678 ft)).

Geographical situation

The central core of the city (Marktplatz, alt. 245 m (804 ft)) lies in the Stuttgart Basin, a trough some 2–3 km (1¼–2 miles) wide, much disturbed by tectonic action, carved out of the local Middle Keuper (Triassic) rocks by the Nesenbach (now largely drained away) and its tributary streams. The basin is open only on the north-east, where it runs into the Neckar Valley; on the south it is bounded by the Keuper hills of Stuttgart-Ostheim, topped here and there by residual hills of the Lower Jurassic (e.g. The Frauenkopf, 462 m (1,581 ft)) and clad on the lower slopes with vineyards, higher up with forest. The western rim of the basin is formed by the Triassic hills of the Glemswald, the sunny slopes of which are also occupied by vineyards.

The city now extends beyond the basin and its enclosing hills, reaching northward into the limestone (Muschelkalk) country of the Neckar Basin with its expanses of loess (Langes Feld, Schmidener Feld), rising in the east to the foothills of the Schurwald with their terraced vineyards and orchards, and extending in the south to the Filder ("fields"), a Lower Jurassic plateau famed for the production of white cabbage.

From within the Federal Republic: 0711
From the United Kingdom: 010 49 711
From the United States or Canada: 011 49 711

Telephone dialling codes

The city covers an area of 20,735 hectares (51,215 acres), of which 5,354 hectares (13,224 acres) are built up, 4,835 hectares (11,942 acres) are forest, 3,592 hectares (8872 acres) are laid out in orchards and gardens, 2,619 hectares (6469 acres) are arable land and vineyards and 488 hectares (1,205 acres) are parks and other open spaces. Stuttgart is thus one of the Federal Republic's largest agricultural, fruit-growing and wine-producing city areas. It has a total extent from north to south of 19·4 km (12 miles), from east to west of 20·4 km (12¾ miles).

Area

Stuttgart is the ninth largest city in the Federal Republic, with a population in June 1984 of 555,572, or some 6 per cent of the population of the *Land* of Baden-Württemburg.

Population

◀ *Schillerplatz, with the Schiller Monument, Stiftskirche and Fruchtkasten*

Stuttgart has the second-largest population of foreigners among the cities of the Federal Republic, coming second to Frankfurt am Main with a total in 1984 of 96,104, including 27,313 Yugoslavs, 17,164 Turks, 15,811 Italians and 14,024 Greeks. The high number of foreigners conceals the fact that since 1959 more than 127,500 Germans have moved out of Stuttgart, though most of them still work in the city. This also explains the high figure of 135,000 commuters who travel in and out every day, creating heavy rush-hour traffic.

City wards

The city is divided for administrative purposes into twenty-three wards (*bezirke*).

The wards in the central area are Stuttgart-Mitte, Stuttgart-Süd (including Kaltental), Stuttgart-West (including Solitude and the Deer and Boar Park), Stuttgart-Nord and Stuttgart-Ost (including Frauenkopf).

The wards in the outer districts are Bad Cannstatt (including Burgholzhof, Sommerrain and Steinhaldenfeld), Birkach (including Schönberg and Kleinhohenheim), Botnang, Degerloch (including Hoffeld), Feuerbach, Hedelfingen (including Lederberg and Rohracker), Möhringen (including Fasanenhof and Sonnenberg), Mühlhausen (including Freiberg, Mönchfeld, Hofen and Neugereut), Münster, Obertürkheim (including Uhlbach), Plieningen (including Steckfeld, Hohenheim and Asemwald), Sillenbuch (including Heumaden and Riedenberg), Stammheim, Untertürkheim (including Luginsland and Rotenberg), Vaihingen (including Büsnau, Rohr and Dürrlewang), Wangen, Weilimdorf (including Bergheim, Giebel, Hausen and Wolfbusch) and Zuffenhausen (including Neuwirtshaus, Rot and Zazenhausen).

Post-war reconstruction

Stuttgart suffered heavy destruction during the Second World War. Of the 150,000 dwellings in the city only 97,550 were habitable at the end of the war. By the end of 1982 a total of 167,850 dwellings had been built or rebuilt, and the process of reconstruction and rehabilitation is continuing. Three particularly spectacular projects are the Schwabenzentrum development (a commercial and administrative centre in Hauptstätter Strasse), the Bohnenviertel improvement scheme (300 dwellings, shops and offices) and the scheme for the rehabilitation and improvement of Bad Cannstatt old town (removal of industry, improvement of housing conditions and shopping facilities).

Population and Religion

Population

Stuttgart's population has increased more than fourfold since 1871, when it numbered 139,578. By 1939, in spite of heavy losses during the First World War, it had reached 496,490. In spite of further losses during the Second World War (particularly owing to bombing) it had recovered by 1950 to 497,677, mainly as a result of the influx of some 135,000 refugees from other parts of Germany – a movement which continued until 1961. In the 1960s the influx of foreign workers (*Gastarbeiter*) began, bringing the city's population to 643,734 in 1962. With increasing prosperity many people (127,500 since 1959) have moved out of the city to more attractive homes in the country areas round the city. In spite of the numerous foreigners who have moved into Stuttgart, now representing some 18 per cent of the population and an establishment element in the city's economic, social and cultural life, the total population has continued to decline since the mid 1960s, while the recession and immigration controls have led to a fall in the number of resident foreigners.

The head of the city's administration is the Chief Burgomaster (Oberbürgermeister), elected by popular vote for a term of eight years, who is chairman of the municipal council. He is assisted by eight full-time deputies, who are elected by the municipal council, also for an eight-year term. The senior deputy acts as the Chief Burgomaster's representative over the whole range of municipal business and has the title of First or Senior Burgomaster. The others, who bear the title of Burgomaster, are responsible for particular departments.

Administration

The municipal council (Gemeinderat) consists of the Chief Burgomaster as chairman and sixty councillors (unpaid) elected by popular vote for a five-year term. It meets in full council or in its numerous committees.

In each of the city's twenty-three wards there is a ward council, with purely advisory and consultative functions, consisting of a chief officer as chairman and from nine to twenty ward councillors according to the size of the ward.

The majority of the city's population (at present 52 per cent) is traditionally Protestant. Roughly a third are Roman Catholics, and some 18 per cent belong to other religious denominations.

Religion

Transport

Since 1 October 1978 the city's transport services – mainly those provided by the German Federal Railways (DBB) and the Stuttgart Tramways (SSB) – have been combined and co-ordinated in the Verkehrs- und Tarifverbund Stuttgart (Transport and Tariff Union).

Local services

The S-Bahn (suburban railway system) runs services between the city centre and Plochingen, Schorndorf, Backnang, Marbach, Bietigheim, Weil der Stadt and Böblingen. A line to Echterdingen Airport is under construction.

The tramway system consists of ten routes with a total length of 115 km (71 miles). The number of passengers carried daily is well over 300,000.

The tramway company's 350 buses run on forty-seven routes with a total length of 612 km (380 miles), carrying over 150,000 passengers every day.

There are a number of country bus routes serving the city's outer districts and the surrounding area.

The tramway company is at present engaged in developing part of its system into a highly modern Stadtbahn (city railway). Prototypes of the new vehicles are already in experimental operation.

Stuttgart's Central Station is an important national and regional junction handling some 200,000 passengers daily. It is at the intersection of two important international routes:

Rail services

Paris – Strasburg – Karlsruhe – Stuttgart – Munich – Salzburg – Vienna – Istanbul and Copenhagen – Hamburg – Würzburg/

A Stuttgart tram

The Neckarhafen

Frankfurt–Stuttgart–Zürich–Milan. There are motorail services from Stuttgart (Kornwestheim) to Narbonne (France), Rimini (Italy), Ljubljana and Rijeka (Yugoslavia), Villach (Austria) and the German North Sea island of Sylt.

Airport

Stuttgart's airport at Echterdingen, 13 km (8 miles) south of the city centre, is used by eleven airlines flying scheduled services as well as by forty charter companies. In 1984 it handled some 2·7 million passengers and 45,000 tonnes of air freight, plus 6,800 tonnes of air mail. More than a million items of mail are carried to and from Stuttgart every night by air.

Port traffic

The city's river port, the Neckarhafen, covers an area of 122 hectares (300 acres) in the wards of Hedelfingen, Untertürkheim and Wangen. The three basins, the construction of which began in 1954, have a total quay length of 5·6 km (3½ miles), and in 1984 the port had a total turnover of some 4 million tonnes. The main types of freight carried are oil products, building materials, corn and animal fodder, steel, iron, scrapmetal and coal.

Motorways and federal highways

A8: Karlsruhe – Stuttgart – Munich (access points: Stuttgart – Vaihingen intersection, Stuttgart – Degerloch, Stuttgart – Flughafen)

A831/A81: Stuttgart – Singen (access point: Stuttgart – Vaihingen intersection)

A81: Stuttgart – Heilbronn (access points: Stuttgart/Leonberg, Stuttgart–Feuerbach, Stuttgart–Zuffenhausen)

B10:	Augsburg – Ulm – Stuttgart – Pforzheim – Karlsruhe – Saarbrücken
B14:	Nürnberg – Schwäbisch Hall – Stuttgart – Rottweil – Stockach
B27:	Würzburg – Heilbronn – Stuttgart – Tübingen – Donaueschingen (Schaffhausen/Switzerland)
B29:	Stuttgart – Nördlingen
B295:	Stuttgart – Calw
B312:	Stuttgart – Reutlingen – Riedlingen/Donau - Memmingen

Motorways (*Autobahnen*) are numbered with the letter A, Federal highways (*Bundesbahnen*) with the letter B.

The "Friendship Road" (Freundschaftsstrasse, Route de l'Amitié) links Germany and France, running from Stuttgart via Wildbad, Freudenstadt, Oberkirch, Kehl, Strasburg, Obernai, Molsheim, Saverne and Sarrebourg to Metz.

"Friendship Road"

Culture

Stuttgart is the principal cultural centre in south-western Germany. It owes this reputation not only to the State Ballet, which became world-famous under the direction of John Cranko and Marcia Haydée, and the Stuttgart Chamber Orchestra under its conductor Karl Münchinger, but also to its numerous theatres with their widely ranging programmes, its fine museums, galleries and archives and its excellent connections with other countries.

General

Stuttgart is one of the six cities in the Federal Republic with the greatest number of higher educational establishments: Stuttgart University (originally established in 1890 as the Technical College); Hohenheim University (which developed out of an agricultural college established in Hohenheim Palace in 1818); the State College of Music and the Dramatic Arts (Staatliche Hochschule für Musik und Darstellende Kunst: originally a private school of music established in 1857 and later taken over by the State, which became in 1865 the Conservatoire of Music, in 1896 the Royal Conservatoire and in 1922 the Württemberg College of Music); the State Academy of Art (originally founded in 1829 as the School of Art and combined in 1941 with the School of Applied Art); Colleges of Technology, Public Administration, Printing and Librarianship; and the Seminary of the Union of Independent Waldorf Schools.

Higher educational establishments

Stuttgart's numerous public and private institutes of scientific research include the Max Planck Institute of Solid State Research, the Max Planck Institute of Research into Metals, the Building Information Centre of the Fraunhofer Society, the Institute of Educational Planning and Information and the Institute of Psychotherapy and Depth Psychology.

Institutes

Stuttgart has three museums of more than regional standing. The ethnological collections of the Linden Museum are among the most important of their kind in Europe; the Württemberg Museum in the Old Palace illustrates the development of culture in Württemberg; and the State Museum of Natural

Museums and galleries

The Stuttgart Ballet has an international reputation

History in Rosenstein Park has a valuable collection of material from southern Germany.

The State Gallery and the City Gallery are widely famed, not least for their fine special collections.

Music and drama

The principal centres of dramatic art in Stuttgart are the Württemberg State Theatres. Names such as Palitzsch, Peymann and Heyme recall the brilliant, but nevertheless controlled, productions put on in the Little House (Kleines Haus) of the State Theatres. The Stuttgart Ballet owes its international reputation to John Cranko and Marcia Haydée.

The literary cabaret of the Renitenz-Theater ("Awkward Theatre") is treasured by connoisseurs as a special delight. International variety stars appear in the new Summer Theatre on the Killesberg. Special mention should also be made of the establishment known as Kultur unterm Turm ("Culture under the Tower"), with the "tri-bühne" and the Stuttgart Puppet Theatre.

Concerts of major importance are given in the Liederhalle. The Württemberg State Orchestra, the Stuttgart Chamber Orchestra under Karl Münchinger, the Stuttgart Radio Symphony Orchestra, the Stuttgart Wind Quintet, the Melos Quartet, the Paul Gerhardt Orchestra, the Stuttgart Philharmonic Orchestra and the Stuttgart Orchestral Union have reputations extending far beyond the boundaries of Württemberg; and among Stuttgart's many choirs the Hymnus Choirboys, the South German Madrigal Choir, the Stuttgart Oratorio Choir, the Württemberg Chamber Choir and the Stuttgart Liederkranz enjoy particular reputation.

One of the leading figures in Stuttgart's musical life is Professor

H. Rilling, whose Gächingen Choir (Gächinger Kantorei) has been acclaimed all over the world. It is largely due to Professor Rilling that Stuttgart now has an International Bach Academy. Entertainment of a more popular kind is provided by Gotthilf Fischer, whose choirs are recruited from outside Stuttgart as well as from the city itself.

Stuttgart is the headquarters of the Institute for Relations with Other Countries (Institut für Auslandsbeziehungen: originally founded in 1917 as the Deutscher Auslandsinstitut). It also has an America House, a French Institute, an Italian Institute and a Yugoslav Information Centre.

The city is twinned with St Helens in England (since 1948), Cardiff in Wales (1955), St Louis in the United States (1960), Strasburg in France (1962), Bombay in India (1968), Menzel-Bourguiba in Tunisia (1971) and Cairo in Egypt (1979).

In addition the Vaihingen and Zuffenhausen districts of the city are twinned with Melun and La Ferté-sous-Jouarre in France. Many part-German part-foreign companies are based in Stuttgart.

Relations with other countries

Commerce and Industry

Stuttgart is one of the Federal Republic's leading industrial and commercial centres, with high levels of pay and attractive working conditions which contribute to the movement of some 135,000 commuters to work in the city every day. It has an employed population of some 420,000, of whom 40 per cent are in the processing industries (including building), just under 60 per cent in the service trades (commerce 15 per cent, transport and communications 7 per cent, financial institutions 6 per cent others about 32 per cent) and 1 per cent in agriculture.

The industrial structure includes a high proportion of growth industries (motor vehicles, electronics, communications technology).

General

A basis for the rapid development of industry in Stuttgart was provided by its importance as Württemberg's leading commercial centre (a consequence of its status as capital), an intelligent and enterprising work-force, much influenced by the values of Protestantism and Pietism, the influx of workers from the poorer agricultural areas and the city's central situation in the Württemberg railway system.

Development

In 1895 the number employed in craft production and industry was 37,000; by 1933 the figure had risen to almost 100,000; and in 1984 there were 121,000 persons employed by 352 firms with 20 or more workers. The total output of the city's industries in 1984 amounted to some 37 billion DM, with exports accounting for 42 per cent.

The numbers employed in various industries at the end of September 1984 were as follows:

Employment

Motor vehicles	45,000
Electronics and electrical engineering	30,000
Engineering	13,000
Precision engineering and optical goods	6,500
Printing and papermaking	5,000
Foodstuffs	4,500
Chemicals	3,500

15

The new headquarters of the Allianz Insurance Corporation (Urbanstrasse/Charlottenstrasse)

Leading firms

Among the best-known firms are Bosch (electrical engineering), Daimler-Benz and Porsche (motor vehicles), Behr (radiators), Mahle (pistons), Transformatoren-Union, Standard-Elektrik-Lorenz (SEL, an affiliate of the American ITT group: electronics), IBM (office machinery, computers), Bleyle and R. & A. Becker (clothing), Kodak and Bosch Photokino (cameras), Matthaes, Pfeiffer and Schiedmayer (pianos).

The Dinkelacker, Leicht (Schwabenbräu) and Stuttgarter Hofbräu breweries, together with the Sanwald brewery (white beer), produce an annual total of more than 2 million hectolitres (44 millon gallons) of beer.

As a publishing centre Stuttgart comes second only to Munich, with 157 publishing houses.

Trade fairs

Stuttgart features prominently in the national and international programme of exhibitions and congresses as the "trade fair centre for the growth industries". Excellent facilities are provided by the Trade Fair Grounds on the Killesberg (with an integrated congress building), the Liederhalle and the Hanns Martin Schleyer Hall.

Among trade fairs of more than regional importance held in Stuttgart are AMB (metal processing), CMT (caravanning, motoring, tourism), ELTEFA (electrical engineering, electronics), Fensterbau (windows), Garten (gardens), Interbad (balneology), Intergastra (hotels, restaurants, confectionery), Intervitis (viticulture and wine production), Intherm (energy technology), ISA (International Collectors' Fair), Optica (optical goods), R (shutters and sun protection) and Sicherheit (security of property and persons).

Stuttgart has a Stock Exchange and a Commodity Exchange. The Landesgirokasse (Provincial Giro Bank), jointly managed by the city and the *Land* of Baden-Württemberg, is the second largest savings bank in the Federal Republic.

Stuttgart is also the headquarters of GENO (the central bank of a federation of savings banks in Württemberg) and the Girozentrale (Württemberg Communal Bank). All the major national banks and a number of large international banks have branches in the city.

Stuttgart is also an important insurance centre, with the offices of such well-known firms as Allianz Leben, Allianz Versicherung, Sparkassenversicherung, Allgemeine Rentenanstalt and Württembergischer Gemeindeversicherungsverein.

Banking and insurance

In 1984 Stuttgart recorded a total of 484,851 visitors, with 1,027,637 bed-nights and an average stay of 2·1 days. The city has a total of some 6,200 beds in just under 150 hotels, guest-houses and pensions.

Tourism

Stuttgart did not develop into a major commercial centre in Württemberg until the 19th c., when, with a growing population and increasing industrialisation, it attracted increasing numbers of commercial firms. Among well-known firms long established in the city are Hahn & Kolb (tools), Marwitz & Hauser (optical goods), Stinnes-Trefz (formerly J. Trefz & Söhne: fuels, fertilisers), E. Breuninger (department store), Coop Schwaben (co-operative: household requirements, etc.) and Nanz (foodstuffs).

Commerce

Stuttgart municipal authority runs the largest market in Baden-Württemberg for animals for slaughter (handling more than 70,000 head in 1983) and the largest slaughtering facilities (23,193 tonnes in 1983).

The Stuttgart Central Market in the Wangen district supplies a population of 4 million in the Middle Neckar Valley and adjoining areas with agricultural produce, fruit and garden produce. The total turnover is some 365,000 tonnes (75 per cent of this total accounted for by imports, half of them from Common Market countries).

Notable Personalities

Willi Baumeister, one of the leading representatives of Abstract painting in Germany, was born in Stuttgart. A pupil of Adolf Hoelzel (see below), he became a professor at the Academy of Art in Stuttgart in 1946.

Willi Baumeister
(1889–1955)

Paul Bonatz, born in Solgne (Lorraine), became Professor of Architecture and Town-planning in the Stuttgart Technical College in 1908. Together with Paul Schmitthenner he established the reputation of the Stuttgart school of architects. His most important building in Stuttgart is the Central Station (see entry).

Paul Bonatz
(1877–1956)

Robert Bosch, an electrical engineer, was born at Albeck, near Ulm. In 1886 he established a precision engineering and electrical engineering plant in Stuttgart, in which high-tension magneto ignition was developed in 1902, giving his firm an international reputation. It is now one of the Federal Republic's leading industrial concerns. Robert Bosch's interest in social and economic problems sometimes made him unpopular with

Robert Bosch
(1861–1942)

Robert Bosch

Gottlieb Daimler

G. W. F. Hegel

his contemporaries; but Stuttgart owes to his initiative the large hospital which bears his name. The Robert Bosch Foundation is particularly concerned with promoting the training of young scientists.

Johannes Brenz
(1499–1570)

The Reformer Johannes Brenz, born in Weil der Stadt, produced the first Protestant Catechism. He played a major part in bringing the Reformed faith to Württemberg, and in 1553 became Provost of the Stiftskirche (see entry) in Stuttgart. Six years later he drew up the Württemberg Church Articles (Grosse Württembergische Kirchenordnung) and founded the Old Württemberg Church.

Carl Eugen,
Duke of Württemberg
(1728–93)

Duke Carl Eugen, a Roman Catholic, was born in Brussels and brought up at the Court of Frederick the Great; he ruled Württemberg from 1744 until his death. An intelligent ruler, interested in art, he gave a powerful stimulus to the cultural life of his country. He founded the Württemberg Library and the Carlsschule, a school for training the country's élite; its most famous pupil was Friedrich Schiller (see entry). His reign saw the building of the New Palace in Stuttgart, Solitude, Monrepos at Ludwigsburg, Hohenheim Palace (see entry) and a palace at Scharnhausen. His second wife, Franziska von Hohenheim, had a moderating influence on his impetuous temperament.

Johann Friedrich, Freiherr
Cotta von Cottendorf
(1764–1832)

Johann Friedrich, Freiherr (Baron) Cotta von Cottendorf, a native of Stuttgart, was proprietor of the Tübingen publishing house of J. G. Cotta and, thanks to his personal relationships with Schiller and Goethe, became the leading publisher of contemporary German literature. He founded the "Allgemeine Zeitung", a newspaper which for many years enjoyed great authority. His firm was taken over in 1889 by the Stuttgart publisher and bookseller Adolf von Kröner.

John Cranko
(1927–73)

Born in Johannesburg (South Africa), John Cranko was from 1961 to 1973 Choreographer of the Stuttgart State Ballet, where he achieved international fame with his new ballet style.

Gottlieb Daimler
(1834–1900)

Gottlieb Daimler, born in Schorndorf, graduated from Stuttgart Polytechnic and in 1883, with Wilhelm Maybach, developed in

Theodor Heuss

Eduard Mörike

Friedrich von Schiller

his experimental workshop in Cannstatt a fast-running internal-combustion engine. In 1890 he established the Daimler Motor Company in Untertürkheim, which in 1926 amalgamated with Carl Benz's company to form the Daimler-Benz Company.

Eberhard continued the building activity of his father Ludwig I, founded Tübingen University in 1477, and in 1482, under the Treaty of Münsingen, secured the reunion of the Stuttgart and Urach parts of the county of Württemberg. In 1495 the Emperor Maximilian granted him the title of Duke.

Eberhard V (Eberhard im Bart), Count (from 1495 Duke) of Württemberg (1445–96)

The Stuttgarter Johann Heinrich von Dannecker, who studied in Paris, Rome and elsewhere, was one of the leading sculptors of the German classical school. His best-known works are in Weimar (bust of Schiller) and Stuttgart (bust of Schiller, self-portrait).

Johann Heinrich von Dannecker (1758–1841)

The Stuttgart-born Jew, Bruno Frank, a friend of Thomas Mann during their years of exile, wrote, among other works, the novel "Trenck" (1926) and the comedy "Sturm im Wasserglas" ("Storm in a Teacup", 1930).

Bruno Frank (1897–1945)

Ferdinand Freiligrath, born in Detmold, wrote poems on social and political themes expressing liberal and democratic ideas, and in consequence was several times driven into exile (in Belgium, Switzerland and Britain). He was co-editor with Karl Marx of the "Neue Rheinische Zeitung", published in Cologne. From 1868 he lived in Stuttgart, later moving to Cannstatt. He translated works by Victor Hugo, Burns and Longfellow.

Ferdinand Freiligrath (1810–76)

Born in Vaihingen an der Enz, Karl von Gerok moved to Stuttgart in 1849 and later became Urban Dean and Principal Preacher to the Court. He wrote patriotic and religious poems (e.g. "The Boy's Prayer").

Friedrich Karl von Gerok (1815–90)

The Stuttgart writer Wilhelm Hauff was a member of the group of Swabian Romantics whose leaders were Uhland and Kerner. He made his name with a historical novel, "Lichtenstein", his tale "Jud Süss" and his fairy-tales ("Kalif Storch", "Zwerg

Wilhelm Hauff (1802–27)

Notable Personalities

Nase", "Das Kalte Herz", "Das Wirtshaus im Spessart"). Some of his writings are to be seen in the National Schiller Museum (see Marbach).

Georg Wilhelm Friedrich Hegel
(1770–1831)

Hegel, a native of Stuttgart, was educated at the Tübinger Stift (a Protestant theological seminary) and devoted himself to the study of theology and philosophy. He was friendly with the poet Hölderlin and the philosopher Schelling. After several years as a private tutor he became, in 1801, a Lecturer at the University of Jena, where he wrote the "Phenomenology of Mind". In 1816 he was a Professor at Heidelberg, and in 1818 moved to Berlin, where his "Philosophy of Justice" (1821) was written. Some of his most important series of lectures, including the "History of Philosophy" and the "Philosophy of Religion", were published only after his death.

On the 200th anniversary of his birth the city of Stuttgart established the Hegel Prize, awarded for outstanding work in the humanities (see Hegel's Birthplace).

Georg Herwegh
(1817–75)

George Herwegh, a native of Stuttgart, published his poems, "Gedichte eines Lebendigen" ("Poems of a Living Man") in Switzerland in 1841–44. Their lively rhetoric helped to prepare the ground for the Revolution of March 1848, in which Herwegh played an active part.

Theodor Heuss
(1884–1963)

Theodor Heuss, born in Brackenheim, became Minister of Education for Württemberg-Baden in 1945–46. He was one of the founders of the Free Democratic Party (FDP). A Professor at the Stuttgart Technical College in 1947–48, he was appointed in 1949 a member of the Parliamentary Council and helped in the drafting of the Basic Law of the Federal Republic. He was elected as the Federal Republic's first President in September 1949 and re-elected in July 1954. After the end of his second term he settled in Stuttgart.

Adolf Hoelzel
(1853–1934)

Hoelzel, born in Olmütz, was a painter of the Realist school who was a Professor at the Stuttgart Academy of Art from 1906 to 1919. His work on the harmony of colours led him to become an Abstract artist.

Max Horkheimer
(1895–1973)

The social philosopher Max Horkheimer, a native of Stuttgart, played a major part in the formation of the Frankfurt school, to which he belonged until 1930 and again from 1949. In 1934 he was appointed Director of the Institute of Social Research in New York. Among his most important works is the "Dialectic of Enlightenment" (1947), written in collaboration with Theodor Adorno.

Aberlin Jörg
(c. 1420–1493/94)

Aberlin Jörg was a busy 15th c. architect who was responsible, among other work, for the nave of the Stiftskirche, the rebuilding of St Leonard's Church, the Dominican Church (known after the Reformation as the Hospital Church) and the alteration and enlargement of the choir and nave of Cannstatt's Town Church.

Isolde Kurz
(1853–1944)

The Stuttgart-born writer Isolde Kurz, daughter of the Reutlingen poet Hermann Kurz, made her name with works which were frequently on Italian Renaissance themes, such as her "Florentiner Novellen" ("Florentine Stories", 1890) and "Italienische Erzählungen" ("Italian Tales", 1895).

The politician Reinhold Maier, born in Schorndorf, near Stuttgart, was from 1924 to 1933 Chairman of the German Democratic Party and a member of the Württemberg Landtag. From 1930 to 1933 he was Minister of Trade and Commerce for Württemberg and in 1932–33 a Member of the Reichstag. In 1945 he founded the Democratic People's Party (DVP), which was later absorbed into the Free Democratic Party (FDP). From 1945 to 1952 he was Prime Minister of Württemberg-Baden and in 1952–53 of the reorganised *Land* of Baden-Württemberg. From 1953 to 1959 he was a member of the Bundestag and from 1957 to 1960 Federal Chairman of the FDP.

Reinhold Maier
(1889–1971)

The explorer Carl Mauch, who was born at Stetten in the Rems Valley and died in Stuttgart, in 1871 discovered the ruins of the legendary ancient settlement of Zimbabwe in southern Africa, from which the new state of Zimbabwe (previously Southern Rhodesia) took its name.

Carl Mauch
(1837–75)

Wilhelm Maybach collaborated with Gottlieb Daimler from 1883, and with him developed a fast-running petrol engine. In 1909, with support from Count Zeppelin, he established the Maybach Motor Company at Friedrichshafen on Lake Constance, at first manufacturing airship engines and later motor cars.

Wilhelm Maybach
(1846–1929)

The Ludwigsburg-born Eduard Mörike, a member of the Swabian school and perhaps the most important poet of the Late Romantic period, taught at the Katharineum in Stuttgart from 1851 to 1866. During this period he wrote his fairy-tale "Das Stuttgarter Hutzelmännlein". Many of his lyrical poems were set to music by leading composers. Some of his writings and other mementoes can be seen in the National Schiller Museum (see Marbach).

Eduard Mörike
(1804–75)

Born in a village near Reichenberg (now Liberec in Czechoslovakia), in 1923 Ferdinand Porsche became Technical Manager of the Daimler-Benz Company in Untertürkheim. In 1931 he established a design office of his own, in which he conceived the legendary Volkswagen in 1934. His Zuffenhausen plant produced, particularly after the Second World War, fast sports cars which soon gained an international reputation.

Ferdinand Porsche
(1875–1951)

The Stuttgart actor, humorist and cabaret artistè Willy Reichert gained enormous popularity for his monologues in Swabian dialect. Particular favourites were his sketches "Herr Häberle and Herr Pfleiderer", performed in conjunction with Oskar Heiler.

Willy Reichert
(1896–1973)

Otto Reiniger, a native of Stuttgart, was one of the leading German outdoor painters. He was trained in Stuttgart, Munich and Italy.

Otto Reiniger
(1863–1909)

Johannes Reuchlin, born in Pforzheim, was Counsellor to Count Eberhard V of Württemberg (see entry) from 1482 to 1496 and a Member of the Court Tribunal. Later he became a lawyer and a judge in the Swabian Federal Court. He ranks with Erasmus of Rotterdam as the leading representative of humanism in Germany.

Johannes Reuchlin
(1455–1522)

Notable Personalities

Claus Schenk, Count von Stauffenberg (1907–44)

Count von Stauffenberg, who was born in Jettingen and grew up in Stuttgart, became a Colonel in the Army Reserve in 1944. After his unsuccessful attempt on Hitler's life on 20 July 1944 he was court-martialled and shot.

Berthold Schenk, Count von Stauffenberg (1905–44)

Like his brother, he grew up in Stuttgart, attending the Eberhard-Ludwigs-Gymnasium (grammar school). After the failure of the attempt on Hitler's life he was executed in Berlin.

Gottlieb Schick (1776–1812)

The Stuttgart painter, a pupil of von Dannecker (see above), was one of the leading representatives of the German classical school, specialising in Biblical and mythological themes. His best portraits are those of Freifrau von Cotta and Frau Dannecker.

Heinrich Schickhardt (1558–1634)

Born in the little town of Herrenberg, near Stuttgart, Heinrich Schickhardt became Chief Architect and Master of Works to the Court and State of Württemberg. He was responsible for the construction of the Prinzenbau and the Fruchtkasten (see entries).

Friedrich von Schiller (1759–1805)

The great poet and dramatist Friedrich von Schiller, born in Marbach (see entry), was required to attend the Carlsschule on the orders of Duke Carl Eugen. He studied law and medicine, and in 1780 became a regimental doctor in Stuttgart. During his student years he read Klopstock, Rousseau and Shakespeare. His concern with the conflict between instinct and intelligence, nature and freedom, was reflected in his play "Die Räuber" ("The Robbers"), which he published at his own expense in 1781. After its first performance in the National Theatre in Mannheim Schiller was forbidden all further poetical activity. In 1782 he left Stuttgart with the musician Andreas Streicher. Schiller's birthplace in Marbach (see entry) is preserved as a memorial. The National Schiller Museum, also in Marbach is devoted to his work.

Oskar Schlemmer (1888–1943)

Oskar Schlemmer, a native of Stuttgart, was a pupil of Hoelzel (see above) at the Stuttgart Academy of Art. As a painter he belonged to the Constructivist school. Having made a name for himself at the Bauhaus in Weimar and Dessau, he fell under the Nazi ban in 1933. There is an Oskar Schlemmer Archive in the State Gallery (see entry).

Paul Schmitthenner (1884–1972)

Born in Lauterbourg in Alsace, Paul Schmitthenner became an architect. From 1918 to 1945 he was a Professor at the Technical College in Stuttgart and, with Paul Bonatz (see above), helped to build up the reputation of the Stuttgart school of architects. His finest buildings in Stuttgart are the Zuffenhausen School (1930) and the Königin-Olga-Bau (1950).

Christian Friedrich Daniel Schubart (1739–91)

Born in Obersontheim, Christian Friedrich Daniel Schubart was Organist and Musical Director to the Württemberg Court in Ludwigsburg from 1769 to 1773. As a writer on political subjects, however, he fell into disfavour and was imprisoned by Duke Carl Eugen on the Hohenasperg from 1777 to 1787. After being pardoned he became Theatrical and Musical Director at the Stuttgart Court.

Gustav Schwab (1792–1850)

The Stuttgart writer Gustav Schwab belonged to the Swabian school centred on the Romantic writers Uhland and Kerner. In addition to songs and novels his works included "The Finest Stories of Classical Antiquity" and the "German Chapbooks". He was co-editor with Adalbert von Chamisso of a literary journal, the "Deutscher Musenalmanach" ("German Almanach of the Muses").

Hans Spemann, son of the Stuttgart publisher Johann Wilhelm Spemann, was awarded a Nobel Prize in 1935 for his work on the development of amphibian embryos.

Hans Spemann
(1869–1941)

Rudolf Steiner, the theosopher and founder of anthroposophy, set up his first school in 1919 at the request of the Manager of the Waldorf-Astoria cigarette factory. It was conceived as an independent comprehensive school, with a twelve-year course, which was to be open to all social classes and run on a collegiate basis. An alternative to traditional patterns of education was to be provided by adjustment of teaching to children's individual capacity, creative activities and the fostering of individual abilities. Out of the Steiner schools there developed son afterwards a rapidly growing movement of Waldorf schools, the centre of which is still Stuttgart (see Uhlandshöhe).

Rudolf Steiner
(1861–1925)

Joseph Süss-Oppenheimer, a Jew from Heidelberg, contrived to find ever-new sources of money for the impecunious Duke Carl Alexander by manipulating the currency and selling offices and privileges. This earned him the rank and style of Privy Councillor; but at the instance of the provincial Estates he was subjected to a trial of doubtful validity, condemned to death and hanged.

Joseph Süss-Oppenheimer
(1692–1738)

The Tübingen poet and lawyer Ludwig Uhland, one of the founders of the Swabian school, was appointed Secretary in the Stuttgart Ministry of Justice in 1810. From 1814 to 1817 he practised as a lawyer in Stuttgart, and in 1819 became a Member of the Chamber of Estates, representing Tübingen. In 1831 he became the representative of Stuttgart in the Landtag, then in opposition to the Government. His papers and mementoes can be seen in the National Schiller Museum (see Marbach).

Ludwig Uhland
(1787–1862)

Friedrich Theodor von Vischer, born in Ludwigsburg, was a friend of Mörike (see entry) and the Swiss writer Gottfried Keller; he became a teacher at the Stuttgart Polytechnic in 1866. As Professor of Aesthetics and German Literature he made a considerable impact with his combative writings, vigorously expressed, and his pantheist philosophy.

Friedrich Theodor von Vischer
(1807–87)

Count von Zeppelin, born in Konstanz, was until 1891 an officer in the Württemberg Army. From 1898 onwards he devoted himself to the construction of airships. In 1908 his airship LZ 4 blew up on what is now Stuttgart's airport at Echterdingen, but a public subscription enabled him to continue with his life's work. He is buried in the Pragfriedhof (see entry).

Ferdinand, Count von Zeppelin
(1838–1917)

History of Stuttgart

Palaeolithic	Earliest settlement within the area of present-day Stuttgart (dated from finds in Neckar, below Cannstatt).
End of Hallstatt Iron Age c. 500 B.C.	Celtic princely grave, with chariot and jewellery (found at Steinhaldenfeld, north of Cannstatt).
A.D. c. 90	Roman fort above the Neckar bend at Cannstatt, on the Neckar section of the *limes*.
3rd–6th c.	The Alemanni occupy land in the Stuttgart district. (Place-names ending in *-ingen*, as Vaihingen, Möhringen and Plieningen, mark their settlements on the fertile land south of the Stuttgart Basin). A cemetery of burials arranged in rows, to the west of the old town centre of Feuerbach, bears witness to a settlement of the Merovingian period.
6th–8th c.	Development of the land by the Franks (with place-names ending in *-heim* and *-hausen*, e.g. Bergheim, Stammheim, Türkheim, Zuffenhausen, Zazenhausen, Mühlhausen).
1020	First mention of a settlement called Frankenbach in the Stuttgart Basin, at the point where an old route crossed the Nesenbach.
1160	Reference to a stud farm called Stükarten, said to have been established by Duke Liudolf about 950. (Hence the horse in the city's coat of arms.)
1229	First documentary reference to Stuttgart.
14th c.	The town becomes the seat of the Counts of Württemberg. The Esslingen suburb and St Leonard's Church are built.
15th c.	A settlement grows up round the Hospital Church, on the pattern of the Italian Renaissance.
1456–58	The first (half-timbered) Town Hall is built.
1463–74	Aberlin Jörg builds St Leonard's Church.
1519	Duke Ulrich, outlawed by the Emperor after serious domestic troubles, is driven out by the Swabian League (a union of the Swabian Estates), who sell Württemberg to the Habsburgs.
1534	Landgrave Philipp of Hesse wins back Württemberg for Ulrich by his victory in the Battle of Laufen. He introduces the Reformed faith with the help of Eberhard Schnepf of Marburg and Ambrosius Blarer of Konstanz. His son Christoph (1550–68) has new articles regulating the Church drawn up by the Swabian Reformer Johannes Brenz (see Notable Personalities).
1553–78	During the reign of Duke Christoph the Old Palace is enlarged by Aberlin Tretsch. Building of the palace church – the first Protestant church in Württemberg.

The Prinzenbau is begun by Heinrich Schickhardt.	1605
Württemberg falls into the hands of the Austrians during the Thirty Years War.	1634–38
Ludwigsburg becomes a royal residence.	1724–33
Building of the New Palace, designed by Leopoldo Retti and Philippe de la Guêpière, which until 1918 remains the residence of the Kings of Württemberg.	1746–97
Building of Monrepos Palace, Ludwigsburg.	1760–66
Duke Carl Eugen (1737–93) again makes Ludwigsburg his residence, while work continues on the New Palace.	1764–75
Foundation of the Military School, later the Carlsschule, at Solitude.	1770
Mineral spring tapped in Cannstatt.	1773
Duke Friedrich II of Württemberg, an Elector since 1803, is raised to the rank of King by Napoleon. Stuttgart becomes capital of the kingdom of Württemberg.	1805
The first railway in Württemberg, between Cannstatt and Esslingen, comes into operation. Later Stuttgart develops into the focal point of the Württemberg railway system, and this gives a powerful stimulus to the town's trade. Industrialisation gets under way.	1845
Opposition to the Government by the middle classes, imbued with liberal and national sentiments, is particularly strong in Stuttgart. Freiligrath, Herweg (see Notable Personalities) and Pfau had prepared the ground for the Revolution of March 1848.	1848–49
Königstrasse, Friedrichstrasse, Schloss-strasse and Neckar-strasse are built. Stuttgart now has a population of some 50,000.	1852
Construction of the Königsbau, in Neo-classical style.	1856–60
Foundation of the "State Collection of Monuments of German Art and Antiquity", later the Württemberg Museum, during the reign of King Wilhelm I.	1862
During the reign of King Karl there is continued building activity.	1864–91
First horse-drawn trams between Stuttgart and Cannstatt.	1868
Gottlieb Daimler and Wilhelm Maybach develop an advanced internal-combustion engine at Cannstatt.	1883
Robert Bosch establishes a precision engineering and electrical engineering workshop, later to develop into a firm of international reputation.	1886
Succeeding the National Liberals who had been dominant	1898

25

	since 1871, the Social Democrats became the strongest political force.
1905	The town of Cannstatt is incorporated in Stuttgart.
1908	The airship LZ 4 blows up on Echterdingen airfield before 50,000 spectators. Degerloch is incorporated in Stuttgart.
1914–27	Paul Bonatz builds Stuttgart's Central Station, one of the great architectural achievements of its day.
1918 (30 Nov.)	Following the example of the Kaiser, King Wilhelm II abdicates.
1924	The South German Radio Company begins operating.
1927	The Weissenhof housing scheme, a pioneering example of modern architecture, is built.
1934	Ferdinand Porsche designs the first of the legendary Volkswagens in Zuffenhausen.
1939–45	Second World War. Almost half the city is destroyed in fifty-three air raids. The worst bombings are on 25–26 July, 12 September and 19 October 1944. The city is occupied by the French on 21 April 1945 and handed over by them to the Americans on 8 July 1945.
1952	Stuttgart, since 1945 capital of the newly created *Land* of Württemberg-Baden, becomes capital of the reorganised *Land* of Baden-Württemberg, the third largest *Land* in the Federal Republic of Germany.
1954–56	Stuttgart acquires a new landmark in the Television Tower, the first of its kind.
1958	Opening of the Wagenburg Tunnel, then the longest road tunnel in Germany (824 m (901 yd)).
1967	The Technical College, much expanded in recent years, becomes Stuttgart University. The Agricultural College at Hohenheim also becomes a university.
1974	Manfred Rommel, a Christian Democrat, becomes Chief Burgomaster.
1981	Six S-bahn (suburban railway) lines link the city centre with the satellite towns of Plochingen, Schorndorf, Backnang, Marbach, Bietigheim and Weil der Stadt. Extensions to Echterdingen Airport and Böblingen are under construction.
1983	European summit in Stuttgart (twenty-sixth meeting of EEC Council).
1984	Opening of new State Gallery.

Sights from A to Z

Academy Garden

See Palace Gardens

Agricultural Museum

See German Agricultural Museum

Arnulf-Klett-Platz

D–G15–18

The square in front of the Central Station, replanned in recent years, is named after Arnulf Klett, who was Chief Burgomaster of Stuttgart from 1945 until his death in 1974.

On the long north-east side of the square stands the Central Station (see entry), facing the Hindenburgbau (by Schmohl, Staehlin and Partners, 1926–28), with arcades designed by Paul Bonatz along its main front, plastered with neon signs. Adjoining it on the west is the Zeppelinbau (1929–31; recently renovated), with offices, shops and the renowned Hotel Graf Zeppelin.

Farther north are the Stuttgart headquarters of the German Federal Railways, surrounded by modern glass-fronted buildings.

Under Arnulf-Klett-Platz is the Klett-Passage (opened in 1976), which links the Central Station with the Central Bus Station (ZOB), the Middle and Upper Palace Gardens (see entry), Königstrasse (see entry) and Lautenschlagerstrasse. In the Klett-Passage are shops with longer-than-usual opening hours, snack-bars, the City Information Centre ("i-punkt"), a Stuttgart Tramways office and a bureau de change of the Landesgirokasse where money can be changed outside the normal hours.

On a lower level, below the shopping arcade, is the Hauptbahnhof (Arnulf-Klett-Passage) U-Bahn (tram) station. On a still lower level is the S-Bahn station of the same name.

U-Bahn
Hauptbahnhof
(Arnulf-Klett-Platz)

S-Bahn
S 1–6 (Hauptbahnhof)

Buses
A, 40, 42, 43

Trams
5, 6, 9, 14, 15

Klett-Passage

*Arts Building

See Kunstgebäude

Asemwald

R13/14

In the Asemwald area – the name probably comes from an old word meaning "cleared forest" – on the plateau to the south of the city centre, between Degerloch and Plieningen, the Neue

Buses
71, 73, 74 (Asemwald)

Bad Cannstatt

Pedestrian zone, Bad Cannstatt

Gottlieb Daimler memorial stone in Kurpark

Distance
5 km (3 miles) south as the crow flies

Heimat ('New Home') firm built between 1968 and 1973 a "machine for living in", complete with every amenity, including an ecumenical community centre and an indoor swimming-pool. Designed by O. Jäger and W. Müller, it consists of three twenty-one-storey slab blocks, set at an angle to one another, which now house some 2,200 people.

Hannibal

It was originally planned to build a huge block of flats, code-named Hannibal, which would have been by far the largest in Europe, but after long and bitter public discussion and controversy the project was dropped in favour of the present scheme.

---

*Bad Cannstatt

D–G15–18

S-Bahn
S 1–3 (Bad Cannstatt)

Buses
52, 55, 56

Trams
1, 2, 13

Boat landing-stage
Wilhelma

Cannstatt, formerly an independent town which was incorporated in Stuttgart in 1905, lies at a Neckar crossing which was already in use in prehistoric times. The origin of the name is unknown.
The earliest traces of human occupation were recently found in the Haas travertine quarry, in the form of a 250,000-year-old hunters' camp. Some years ago a princely tomb of the Hallstatt period (Iron Age) was found at Steinhaldenfeld. Above the Neckar bend the Romans (see Roman Lapidarium) built a fort (in the street called Auf der Steig) which formed part of the *limes* along the line of the Neckar (1st and 2nd c.). Evidence of an Alemannic settlement is provided by a number of burials. In Merovingian times there were a number of hamlets within the

area of Cannstatt; one such settlement has been identified at the Uffkirche.

Cannstatt first appears in the records in 708. It received its municipal charter in 1330, during the reign of Ludwig the Bavarian. The town prospered, thanks to its situation at the meeting-place of routes from Upper Swabia, Augsburg, Speyer, Heilbronn and Alsace and to its wine production.

There was a bathing establishment in Cannstatt as early as 1377, but it was only in the 19th c. that its abundant mineral springs were fully exploited and the town became known as a spa. The reign of King Wilhelm I saw the building of the Kursaal, Rosenstein Palace (see entry) and the Wilhelma Gardens (see entry) on the other side of the Neckar.

The construction of the railway to Esslingen, Stuttgart and Ludwigsburg in the mid 19th c. marked the beginning of a period of rapid industrialisation, which was to lead to a considerable expansion of the town and to its early union with Stuttgart. In 1933 Cannstatt was granted official status as a spa and the right to the prefix "Bad".

See Cannstatt Fair.
See Cannstatter Wasen.
See State Mint.

*Town Church (Protestant)

E15

The three-aisled Town Church (Stadtkirche) in the centre of Cannstatt old town is a Late Gothic hall-church, built between 1460 and 1471 by Aberlin Jörg and enlarged by Heinrich Schickhardt in 1612–13. The vaulted roof was destroyed by lightning in 1790. Restoration of damage suffered during the Second World War was completed by 1965. During the renovation work the church acquired fine modern stained-glass windows (by Kohler) depicting Christ.

Location
Marktplatz

*Gottlieb Daimler Memorial

E16

The Gottlieb Daimler Memorial, to the south of the Kurpark, commemorates the life and work of the great Swabian inventor. Daimler acquired the property in 1882 and built the experimental workshop in which he developed the first fast-running petrol engine. In 1884 he drove his epoch-making vehicle for the first time in the garden of the house.

The workshop and garden were converted some years ago into a small museum.

See Daimler-Benz Museum.

Location
Taubenheimstrasse 13

Opening times
Apr.–Oct., daily 11 a.m.–4 p.m.

Tram
2 (Kursaal)

*Kursaal and Kurpark

E16/17

In 1773 an abundant mineral spring, the Wilhelmsbrunnen, was tapped in Cannstatt. In 1825 King Wilhelm I of Württemberg had a Kursaal built by his Court Architect Nikolaus Thouret, consisting at first only of the present central range preceded by a portico. Later came the north and south wings, the porter's lodge and various offices, together with a passage to the Brunnenhof (Spring Court), with the Gottlieb Daimler Spring (drilled in 1932). In 1906 A. Eitel was commissioned to replace the old restaurant building by the Small Kursaal, which was completed in 1908. The Small Kursaal (renovated) is now linked with the Great Kursaal by a structure of copper and glass.

Kursaal

Bad Cannstatt

Kursaal and monument to King Wilhelm I, Cannstatt

The Kursaal complex, which includes modern conference rooms, a café, a wine bar and a restaurant, has become a very popular rendezvous, various musical events arranged by the Tourist Office providing an additional attraction.

Kurpark

The 17 hectare (42 acre) Kurpark, with a Music Garden, lying for the most part on the slopes of the Sulzerrain, is attractively laid out, with well-cared-for deciduous trees.
To the south is the Gottlieb Daimler Memorial (see above).

Marktplatz and Marktstrasse   E/F15/16

The Marktplatz (Market Square) and part of Marktstrasse are at present in course of rehabilitation under an improvement scheme. Features of interest are the Town Church (see above), the Town Hall of 1491 (now the District Offices) in the Marktplatz, the Erbsenbrunnen ('Pea Fountain'; by Graevenitz, 1929) in Marktstrasse and the Klösterle (Marktstrasse 71), a Beguine house (renovated) of the late medieval period.
Every year in early summer the popular Cannstatt Brezel Festival is held in the Marktplatz and Marktstrasse.

*Uffkirche   F16

Location
Waiblinger Strasse 66

Trams
1, 13 (Uff-Kirchhof)

The area round the Uffkirche was the site of a settlement of the Merovingian period. The church itself first appears in the records in the 13th c. The present church dates from the 15th c. and still has Romanesque details as well as Gothic features. On the outside walls are handsome tombstones.

Two tombs in the churchyard are particularly notable – those of the poet Ferdinand Freiligrath, with a bust by Donndorf (1878), and the car-manufacturer Gottlieb Daimler and his family.

*Wilhelmsplatz

This busy square, completely remodelled in recent years, is named after King Wilhelm I of Württemberg, a great patron of Cannstatt. The dominant feature of the square is the Wilhelms-Center, a complex of shops and offices.
Near by, at Wilhelmstrasse 7, is the Cannstatt Museum (Heimatmuseum: open Wed. 3–5 p.m., Sat. and Sun. 10 a.m.–12 noon).

---

*Bärensee

The principal feature of the Glemswald (see entry) recreation area is the Bärensee (Bears' Lake: alt. 422 m (1,384 ft)), with the Bärenschlössle, the Hirschwiese (Stags' Meadow) and the Rot- und Schwarzwildpark (Deer and Boar Park). The lake is one of the three (the others being the Neuer See and the Pfaffensee) which make up the Glems artificial lake or reservoir (over 2 km (1¼ miles) long, up to 15 m (50 ft) deep), the creation of which was ordered by Duke Christoph in 1566 in order to improve Stuttgart's water-supply.

Buses
85, 93 (Schattengrund)

Distance
6 km (4 miles)

The Bärenschlössle (Bears' Castle) above the east shore of the lake was built in 1768 for the accommodation of high

Bärenschlössle

The Bärensee . . .   *. . . and one of its bears*

personages watching the Duke's hunting-parties in the Glemswald. After being badly damaged during the Second World War it has been restored as a place of refreshment for visitors.

From the Bärenschlössle there is a good view of the Hirschwiese (Stags' Meadow) on the opposite side of the lake, to which beaters drove the game during the Ducal hunting-parties.

Deer and Boar Park

To the east of the Bärenschlössle extends the Deer and Boar Park (Rot- und Schwarzwildpark), with enclosures in which visitors can watch roe deer, red deer, wild boar and other wildlife. A nature trail initiates visitors into the natural history of the Glemswald.

Berg Church   G15

Location
Klotzstrasse 21

Trams
1, 2, 14 (Mineralbäder)

The Neo-Gothic church (the Protestant parish church) of Berg stands on a 40 m (130 ft) high spur of rock above the left bank of the Neckar near the Leuze spa establishment (Mineralbad Leuze). Designed by the Court Architect, Gaab, it was built in the latter part of the 19th c. to replace an older church, first referred to in the 13th c., which was pulled down in 1853. After suffering damage in the last war it was rebuilt in 1955. During the Middle Ages the immediate surroundings of the church were fortified.

Bessarabian Germans, Museum of the   H15
(Heimatmuseum der Deutschen aus Bessarabien)

Location
Florianstrasse 17

Bus
42 (Ostendplatz)

Tram
4 (Ostendplatz)

Opening times
Mon.–Fri. 8.30 a.m.–4 p.m.
Sat. and Sun. by
appointment

This museum, devoted to the life of the German settlers in Bessarabia (now part of the Soviet Union) who were expelled from their homes in 1940, was founded in 1952 and considerably enlarged in 1975. It contains more than 40,000 family records, illustrative material, a library, historical maps and plans of towns and villages, together with models of farmhouses, churches and public buildings and household equipment and textiles. The museum gives an excellent picture of the economic and social structure of the German communities in Bessarabia.

---

*Bible Museum (Bibelmuseum)   P9

Location
Bibelhaus Stuttgart,
Balinger Strasse 31
Stuttgart-Möhringen

Buses
72, 87 (Möhringen
Bahnhof)

Trams
5, 6 (Möhringen Bahnhof)

In this museum is displayed the collection of historic editions of the Bible assembled by the Württemberg Bible Society (Württembergische Bibelanstalt, founded 1818). The museum's principal treasure is a Luther Bible of 1545 with woodcuts from the studio of Lucas Cranach. Other notable items are Hebrew, Greek and Latin Bibles, medieval picture Bibles, a very fine 18th-c. Bible (Pietism) and several mission Bibles. The collection also includes copies of the Dead Sea manuscripts, other translations of the Bible and material showing how the Bible came into being.
Opening times: Mon.–Fri. 8 a.m.–4 p.m.

Summit of the Birkenkopf: a reminder of the bombing

Birkenkopf ("Monte Scherbelino")   L9

The Birkenkopf is a hill on the south-western perimeter of the
Stuttgart Basin which archaeological finds have suggested
was the site of a settlement in the Mesolithic period. The hill,
originally 471 m (1,545 ft) high, was increased in height to
511 m (1,677 ft) when it was used after the last war for the
deposit of 15 million cu. m (20 million cu. yd) of rubble from the
ruins of buildings destroyed by bombing.

The hill's nickname of Monte Scherbelino is a joke-formation
(from *scherbe*, "potsherd") modelled on Monte Testaccio in
Rome, which was built up from shreds of antique pottery.

From the hill there are very fine views. On the summit plateau
is a memorial commemorating the horrors of the Second
World War.

Buses
50, 92 (Birkenkopf)

Distance
3·5 km (2 miles) as the crow
flies

Bismarck Tower (Bismarckturm)   G11

The building of the Bismarck Tower, on the highest point on the
Feuerbacher Heide (409 m (1,342 ft)), was initiated by the
student body of Stuttgart in 1903–04. Even without climbing
the tower visitors can enjoy an attractive view of the city.

Buses
43, 50 (Am Bismarckturm)

Opening times
At present closed

Bohnenviertel   J/K13(T20/21)

Between Charlottenplatz (see entry) in the north and

Bopser

Location
Charlottenstrasse,
Olgastrasse

U-Bahn
Charlottenplatz

Buses
41, 42, 43, 44, 73, 74, 75,
76, 77, 7600
(Charlottenplatz)

Trams
1, 2, 4, 5, 6, 15
(Charlottenplatz)

Katharinenplatz in the south extends part of the old slum quarter known as the Bohnenviertel (Bean Quarter), which has been cleared and improved in recent years. The old slum dwellings have given place to 300 flats for letting or sale, including some designed for students and old people, together with shops, offices and places of refreshment. The Schellenturm (see entry), a relic of the old fortifications, has also been restored.

In Katherinenplatz stands the English Church (1868), designed by Professor Wagner, in which Anglican services are held.

In Charlottenstrasse, facing the new Bohnenviertel development, are the new offices of the Allianz Insurance Corporation, a fine example of modern functional architecture with a very attractive façade.

Bopser L/M13/14

Location
Hoher Bopser,
Bopserklinge,
Bopser Gardens,
Weissenburg Park

Buses
73, 74, 75, 76, 77, 7600
(Bopser)

Trams
5, 6 (Bopser)

From the Hoher Bopser (482 m (1,581 ft)), on top of which is the Television Tower (see entry), a path (the Bopserklinge) descends to the Bopser Gardens (Bopseranlage) and Weissenburg Park (see entry), at the upper end of the Neue Weinsteige (see entry). From these two parks, half-way up the hill, there are attractive views of the city centre.

In the Bopser Gardens stand the Bopser Fountain (Bopserbrunnen) and a monument to the economist Friedrich List, a native of Reutlingen (south of Stuttgart).

The Bopserwaldstrasse, to the east of the Bopserklinge, traverses a select residential area.

Calwer Strasse

Calwer Passage

Fruit Column

Brewery horse

Botanic Gardens

See Hohenheim
See Wilhelma Gardens

*Calwer Strasse   J12(S/T19)

The upper part of Calwer Strasse, which takes its name from the
Calwer Gate (Calwer Tor), which was pulled down in 1836,
has in recent years been rehabilitated in an exemplary
improvement scheme, with full regard to the needs of
conservation. Much of the success of this scheme is due to the
architects Walter Belz and Hans Kammerer, whose designs for
the new offices of the Allegemeine Rentenanstalt (1978) and
the Calwer Passage, a covered shopping arcade, are outstanding examples of modern urban architecture. A number of 18th
and 19th c. houses and shops were renovated under the
improvement scheme.
At the west end of Calwer Strasse is Rotebühlplatz (see entry).

S-Bahn
S 1–6 (Stadtmitte)

Bus
43 (Rotebühlplatz)

Trams
2, 4, 14 (Rotebühlplatz)

Calwer Passage

Cannstatt

See Bad Cannstatt

* Cannstatt Fair (Cannstatter Volksfest)   F/G16

Location
Cannstatter Wasen

S-Bahn
S 1–3 (Bad Cannstatt)

Buses
56, E (Neckarstadion)

Trams
14 (Mineralbäder)
1, 2 (Mercedesstrasse)

Opening times
End Sept.–beginning Oct.,
Mon.–Fri. 11 a.m.–9 p.m.,
Sat. and Sun. 11 a.m.–
11 p.m.

The Cannstatt Fair is the most popular in Swabia and one of the largest of its kind in the world. It is held annually at the end of September and beginning of October on the Cannstatter Wasen (see entry), to which 4 million visitors are attracted every year by more than five dozen fairground attractions, ranging from old favourites such as the Big Wheel to more modern developments like the Looping Star, together with gigantic beer tents, sideshows and shooting-galleries, almond-roasting stalls and pizza bakeries, and countless other attractions.

The first Cannstatt Fair was held on 28 September 1818 under the patronage of King Wilhelm I, and took the form of an agricultural festival. This tradition is maintained in the Agricultural Fair which is held every three years simultaneously with the main fair. The symbol of the Cannstatt Fair is the "Fruit Column", first devised by Nikolaus Thouret in 1818; the column, a symbol of harvest thanksgiving, is richly decorated with fruit.

The most memorable Cannstatt Fair was the one held in 1857, shortly after the Crimean War, when Tsar Alexander II of Russia and his wife, the Emperor Napoleon III of France and the Queens of the Netherlands and Greece all visited the fair on the invitation of the King of Württemberg.

Cannstatter Wasen (Cannstatt Meadow)   F/G16/17

S-Bahn
S 1–3 (Bad Cannstatt)

Bus
56 (Neckarstadion)

Trams
1, 2 (Mercedesstrasse)
14 (Mineralbäder)

The Cannstatter Wasen (Cannstatt Meadow) is an area of open space extending south from Bad Cannstatt along the right bank of the Neckar. Within this area are the Neckar Stadium (see entry) with its Sports Hall, the Hanns Martin Schleyer Hall (see entry), the Festwiese Stadium, tennis-courts, a roller-skating rink, a riding-school, a number of club grounds and other sports facilities, a camping site and the fair ground, which has recently been refurbished and improved.

The Cannstatt Fair (see entry) is held on the Wasen every year in September–October.

* * Central Station (Hauptbahnhof)   H13(R20)

Location
Arnulf-Klett-Platz

U-Bahn
Hauptbahnhof
(Arnulf-Klett-Platz)

S-Bahn
S 1–6 (Hauptbahnhof)

Buses
A, 40, 42, 43
(Hauptbahnhof/Arnulf-
Klett-Platz)
73, 74, 75, 76, 84, 85, 87,
92, 93, 7600, 7945, 7950
(Hauptbahnhof/ZOB)

Trams
5, 6, 9, 14, 15
(Hauptbahnhof/Arnulf-
Klett-Platz)

Stuttgart's Central Station in Arnulf-Klett-Platz (see entry), built between 1914 and 1927 under the direction of Paul Bonatz and E. F. Scholer, is one of the outstanding achievements of modern architecture in the city and one of its most notable landmarks. Its function as a major terminus (and at the time of its erection the focal point of the Württemberg railway network) and its consequent role as a gateway are reflected in its architecture – its cubic structure, housing two monumental entrance halls, and its 56 m (184 ft) high tower on the line of Königstrasse. In building the station Bonatz used what were then the new materials of concrete and steel, but faced the structure with rusticated and dressed limestone blocks.

The station, measuring 200 m (220 yd) from side to side, has eight platforms and sixteen lines. In addition to the necessary traffic control and other installations it houses the Inter-City Hotel in the west wing. Features of artistic interest are the "Swabian Knight" (by Jakob Brüllmann) above the steps leading from the main ticket hall to the platforms and, over the central concourse, the coat of arms from the Royal Gate (Königstor) which from 1810 to 1922 served as the entrance to Königstrasse.

Central Station

The largest signal-box on the Federal Railway system came into operation in the Central Station in 1977. From this control post all train movements and shunting operations can be kept under surveillance.

A little way north-west of the station is the Kriegsberg Tower (Kriegsbergturm), recently reopened to the public, from the top of which there are fine views in all directions.

Kriegsberg Tower

Charlottenplatz

J13(S/T20)

Charlottenplatz, one of the most important traffic intersections in the city centre, was created by the demolition of the old Esslingen Gate and part of the Esslinger Vorstadt (suburb). It is named after the Bavarian Princess Charlotte, King Wilhelm I's first wife, who later married Emperor Franz of Austria. On the west side of the square is the Old Orphanage (see entry), on the north side the Academy Garden (part of the Palace Gardens (see entry)), beyond which are the State Archives and the Württemberg Library (see entries). On the south side the modern Charlottenbau stands on the site of the old Ministry of War, where Wilhelm Hauff (see Notable Personalities) wrote his "Mann im Mond" ("Man in the Moon") and his historical novel "Lichtenstein". Farther south can be found the Bohnenviertel (see entry).

U-Bahn
Charlottenplatz

Buses
41, 42, 43, 44, 73, 74, 75, 76, 77, 7600

Trams
1, 2, 4, 5, 6, 15

* Daimler-Benz Museum

H18

The Daimler-Benz Museum offers an interesting survey of the development of the automobile from its beginnings to the present day. The collection assembled here, in the world's first

Location
Mercedesstrasse 136,
Stuttgart-Untertürkheim

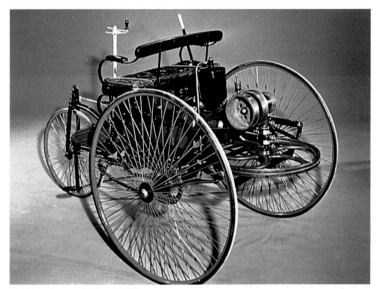

The Benz three-wheeler of 1886

A Mercedes sports car of 1927

automobile factory, ranges from the first two cars every built – the Benz three-wheeler and the Daimler motor carriage of 1886 – to the very latest developments, and includes engines for other land vehicles as well as for ships and aircraft.

In the entrance hall can be seen a display of the current range of models. In a separate area are a series of exhibits illustrating the development of the automobile, including the Daimler motor carriage, the Benz three-wheeler and Daimler's tramcar and motor-boat. Also to be seen here are vehicles illustrating the various stages of development down to 1926, when the Daimler and Benz firms amalgamated.

On the first floor are vehicles produced from 1926 onwards, including robust utility models, luxurious cars with supercharged engines, the world's first mass-produced diesel-engined private car, and cars which belonged to monarchs and heads of state. On the second floor are racing and record-breaking cars, the famous "Silver Arrows" which have established their place in the history of the automobile. Mercedes cars were particularly successful in 1934–39 and again in 1952–55.

S-Bahn
S 1 (Neckarstadion)

Bus
56 (Daimler-Benz)

Tram
23 (Schlotterbeckstrasse)

Opening times
At present closed; for information tel. 0711/ 17 25 78

Degerloch

M–O10–14

In earlier days Degerloch (a name meaning "dense forest"), which was incorporated in Stuttgart in 1908, was a place for changing horses on the steep ascent of the Alte Weinsteige. With the construction of the Neue Weinsteige and the rack railway (see Weinsteige) Degerloch became an attractive residential and recreation area: indeed it acquired official recognition in the 19th c. as an "altitude resort". Handsome villas were built here, but at the same time an extensive network of footpaths was laid out. Some years ago the old centre of the town was the subject of an improvement scheme directed towards the conservation of its older buildings, including the Ritter Inn, a reproduction of a Baroque half-timbered building of the early 18th c.

Within the territory of Degerloch is the Television Tower (see entry), below which is the Waldau (see entry) sports and recreation area. Below Degerloch to the west is the Forest Cemetery (see entry).

Buses
A, 70, 71, 73, 74, 75, 76, 77, 7600

Trams
5, 6, 10

Distance
3 km (2 miles) as the crow flies

Design Centre

See Landesgewerbeamt

Eberhardskirche

See St Eberhard's Church

Eberhardstrasse

J/K12/13(T19/20)

Eberhardstrasse, which bounds the old town centre on the south-east, is named after Count Eberhard V of Württemberg (b. Urach 1445, d. Tübingen 1496).

U-Bahn
Rathaus

Eichenhain

Buses
41, 42, 43, 44, 84, 85, 87,
92, 93, 7945 (Rathaus)

Trams
1, 2, 4

The tradition of this old shopping street has been maintained
with the renovation (by the Stuttgart architect Walter Sorg,
1982) of an older office block, the Graf-Eberhard-Bau (1908),
and the resulting establishment of numbers of exclusive and
specialist shops and traditional-style bars and restaurants.
Behind the Graf-Eberhard-Bau is the attractive Hans-im-Glück
(Lucky Jack) Fountain, by Joseph Zeitler (1909).

Eichenhain O/P15

Location
Stuttgart-Riedenberg/
Stuttgart-Sillenbuch

Buses
65, 70 (Riedenberg)

Tram
15 (Sillenbuch)

Distance
4 km (2½ miles) south-
south-east as the crow flies

Eichenhain (Oak Grove), formerly used as grazing for young
horses, is now designated as a nature reserve. Its handsome
oaks and beeches, several hundred years old, and its scanty
covering of grass are reminiscent of the steppe-like moorland
of the Swabian Alb, whose steeply scarped slopes rise some
25 km (15 miles) to the south. In the Eichenhain is a finely
carved monument (1955) to Elly Heuss-Knapp, wife of
President Theodor Heuss (see Notable Personalities).
The Eichenhain is particularly beautiful with its autumn
colouring, when its attracts many visitors, particularly older
people.

---

* Esslingen

Information
Kultur- und Freizeitamt/
Stadtinformation,
Marktplatz 16,
7300 Esslingen,
tel. 3 51 12 41

S-Bahn
S 1 (Esslingen)

Buses
35, 7677

Distance
12 km (7½ miles) south-east

History

The former Imperial Free City of Esslingen, situated at an
altitude of 240 m (787 ft) upstream from Stuttgart in the Neckar
Valley, was involved from a very early stage in the industrialisation of the Middle Neckar area. It now has a population of just
under 100,000. In spite of the town's stormy history it has
preserved its medieval core, with Gothic, Renaissance and
Baroque burghers' houses, craftsmen's dwellings along the
canals and the old town walls.
Present-day Esslingen, with a famous technical college and a
number of well-known industrial firms (Sektkellerei Kessler,
Hengstenberg), has now joined up with the Stuttgart districts
of Hedelfingen and Obertürkheim to form a continuous built-
up area.

Bronze Age remains found here show that the site was already
occupied about 1000 B.C. In Roman times there was a villa
(farm) at Oberesslingen. The first mention of the town, situated
at a ford on the Neckar, on the old trade route between the
Rhine and Italy, appears in the records in 777. During the
Investiture Conflict (between the Emperor and the Pope over
the appointment of bishops) Esslingen was destroyed by the
troops of the Emperor Henry IV. It received its municipal charter
in 1219. Hostility between the Imperial Free City and the Count
of Württemberg led to inter-city wars from 1246 onwards,
ending in the defeat of Esslingen in 1454. In 1488 the Swabian
League was formed here. In 1531 the municipal council
resolved to allow preaching by Protestants, and the Reformed
faith was brought to Esslingen by Ambrosius Blarer. During the
Thirty Years War and the invasions by French forces in the latter
part of the 17th c. the town suffered severely. In 1803 it lost its
status as an Imperial Free City and became part of Württem-

Esslingen's Marktplatz and Castle

berg. During the Second World War the town – which had grown considerably in size as a result of industrialisation and the incorporation of adjoining communities – was largely unscathed.

In the course of its history Esslingen achieved particular reputation as a wine-producing town. In the 14th c. its wine (Esslinger) was much esteemed not only in Augsburg but as far afield as Salzburg and Vienna. In those days the unit of measurement for wine in both Württemberg and Bavaria was the "Esslingen bucket" (*Eimer*). In the 19th c. there were still several hundred hectares of vineyards within the town's boundaries; now there are only 92 hectares (227 acres).

Wine

All Saints Chapel

To the south of St Dionysius's Church is the old All Saints Chapel (Allerheiligenkapelle), the foundations of which date from the 13th c. It was remodelled by Heinrich Schickhardt in 1610 and how houses the municipal archives, with almost 9,000 documents on parchment.

Location
Marktplatz 20

Old Neckar Bridge

The Old Neckar Bridge, with its massive tower, links the old part of the town (Altstadt) with Pliensau, once an island in the Neckar. The bridge's foundations were laid down in the 13th c.,

Location
Altstadt-Pliensau

but most of the original structure was destroyed by 19th and 20th c. alterations to meet the needs of traffic.
The Pliensau Tower was built in 1280.

*Old Town Hall

Location
Rathausplatz

The Old Town Hall (Altes Rathaus) on the south side of Rathausplatz is a half-timbered building of 1430 which was rebuilt by Heinrich Schickhardt in 1586–89 and provided with a Renaissance façade. A particularly fine feature is the astronomical clock (1592) by Jacob Diem of Tübingen, with a carillon of 1926. The excellent Municipal Museum is housed in the Renaissance entrance hall. The fine council chamber (Bürgersaal) dates from about 1430.
In front of the building is the 14th c. Market Fountain, remodelled in modern style by Fehrle.

Courthouse

Location
Ritterstrasse 8

This building on the banks of the picturesque Rossneckar, originally the Town Hall and from 1803 the Courthouse, was built by J. J. Börel and P. Joachim in 1705–15 to replace an earlier building destroyed by fire in 1701. The two staircases are particularly fine. The Imperial Hall (Kaisersaal) has good stucco decoration and a ceiling-painting by Paul Ambrosius Reith (1726–27).

*Castle

The Castle (Burg), which tops a vine-clad hill on the north side of the town, was built during the Hohenstaufen period (rusticated masonry). Only parts of the structure survive. Notable features are the Dicker Turm (Fat Tower), which now houses a restaurant, the Hohwacht and the Seilergang (Ropewalk).

*St Dionysius's Church

Location
Marktplatz

The twin-towered church of St Dionysius or Town Church (Protestant), situated in the oldest part of the town, was built in the 13th–14th c. in the transitional style of the period, on 8th c. foundations; the choir is in High Gothic style. Excavations inside the church in 1960–63 brought to light the remains of earlier churches, a crypt and a dwelling belonging to the Urnfield culture; visitors can see the excavations (Catacomb Museum).
The magnificent stained glass in the choir came mainly from Esslingen workshops. The High Altar was the work of Peter Riedlinger and David Mieser (1604; restored 1982); it shows scenes from the life of Christ. The rood-screen, the tabernacle and the font are attributed to Lorenz Lechler of Heidelberg (15th c.).

*Weil Manorhouse O20

Weil Manorhouse (Domäne Weil), situated north-west of the town on the left bank of the Neckar bend, is first mentioned in

Old Town Hall

St Paul's and St Dionysius's

the records as an inhabited place in 1173. During the 14th c. it became a centre of mystical thought. In 1643 and 1796 it fell a victim to the wars of the time; then in 1817 King Wilhelm I of Württemberg had a Neo-classical country house built on the site, complete with stud farm and dairy. The architect was Giovanni Salucci, who also designed the burial chapel on the Württemberg (see entry). The house was beautifully restored in 1969–72.

*Frauenkirche

Outside the line of the old town walls, to the north, is the High Gothic Frauenkirche (Church of Our Lady; Protestant parish church), with a magnificent tower (after 1398) designed by Ulrich von Ensingen, architect of Ulm Cathedral. The choir has fine 14th c. stained glass from Esslingen workshops. In the nave are figures of Apostles, on the south-east doorway the life of the Virgin (*c.* 1350), on the south-west doorway the Last Judgment (*c.* 1400).

Location
Augustinerstrasse

Hafenmarkt

This square in the centre of the old town has had a long and eventful history. In the square are the four oldest half-timbered houses in the Federal Republic (Nos. 4, 6, 8 and 10; all 14th c.). The Yellow House (Gelbes Haus) is a well-preserved tower house of the second half of the 13th c.

Innere Brücke

The medieval Innere Brücke (Inner Bridge) spans the picturesque Wehrneckar, the Maille (an island in the Neckar, now laid out as a park) and the Rossneckar. On the bridge stands the Gothic St Nicholas's Chapel (first recorded in 1350), which was re-dedicated in 1959 as a memorial to the victims of National Socialism.

In Archivstrasse is the Postmichelbrunnen (Postman Fountain).

Landratsamt

Location
Ritterstrasse 10

The Landratsamt (District Council Office) has been housed since the 19th c. in this palace which was built in the Baroque style of Upper Swabia (designed by Matthias Widmann, 1722–25), replacing an earlier house burned down in 1701.

* New Town Hall

Location
Rathausplatz 2

On the north side of Rathausplatz is the Baroque New Town Hall (Neues Rathaus), also known as the Palmsches Palais. It was built in 1748 for Franz, Freiherr (Baron) von Palm, an Imperial Councillor.

Pfleghöfe

The Pfleghöfe were hospices belonging to the four Mendicant Orders and other religious houses, established in the important wine-producing town of Esslingen.

The Salmannsweiler Pfleghof (Untere Beutau 8), facing the east end of the Frauenkirche, is a massive building with rusticated masonry dating from the Hohenstaufen period.

The Speyerer Pfleghof (Marktplatz 21–23) was built in the 13th c. and enlarged in the 16th. It is now occupied by the Sektkellerei Kessler, the oldest producer of sparkling wine in Germany (established 1826).

The Fürstenfelder Pfleghof (Strohgasse 13) was built in the early 18th c.

The Kaisheimer Pfleghof (Burgsteige 1–3), known as the Klösterle, shows Rococo as well as Late Gothic features.

The Konstanzer Pfleghof (Webergasse 3) was founded in 1327.

St Paul's Church

Location
Marktplatz

On the west side of the Marktplatz stands St Paul's Church (Roman Catholic parish church), built between 1233 and 1268. It is the oldest surviving vaulted church belonging to a Mendicant Order (in this case the Dominicans).

The 15th c. Madonna on the east pier was formerly in the Frauenkirche. There is a fine Late Gothic Crucifix over the High Altar.

Kielmeyer House

Location
Marktplatz

This magnificent half-timbered house on foundations of rusticated stonework dominates the north side of the Marktplatz. It is the last remnant of the large hospice which once stood here, originally housing the hospice's wine-press. At the south-west corner, under the cornice on the first floor, is an old figure, the "Teufele" (Little Devil), holding a shield with the date 1582.

Theatre

The ultra-modern Theatre (Schauspielhaus), opened in 1982, is the home of the Württemberg Theatre Company, the successor to a company established in 1804.
The new theatre (with seats for 460), designed by Hans-Rolf Sommer, is reminiscent of Hans Scharoun's Philharmonic Hall in Berlin, but fits well into its surroundings.

Location
Strohstrasse

Wolfstor

The Wolfstor (Wolf's Gate) on the south-eastern boundary of the old town, is first mentioned in the records in 1268 and is one of the last relics of the town walls of the Hohenstaufen period. The lions (heraldic animals of the Hohenstaufens), in Late Romanesque style, are well preserved.

Location
Küferstrasse

Eugensplatz   J13

Eugensplatz, named after Duke Eugen of Württemberg (b. 1846, d. Düsseldorf 1877) lies on a terrace above the east side of the old town.
The bronze figure on the Galatea Fountain (Galateabrunnen; by Rieth, 1890) depicts the beautiful nymph of Greek mythology, and created some sensation when first unveiled.

Bus
42 (Eugensplatz)

Tram
15 (Eugensplatz)

Fangelsbach Cemetery (Fangelsbachfriedhof)   K/L12

Fangelsbach Cemetery, in the south of the city, was laid out in 1823. Notable among the tombs it contains are those of the philosopher Immanuel Hermann von Fichte (1796–1879), the great architect Nikolaus Friedrich von Thouret (1767–1845) and the industrialist Gustav Siegle (1840–1905).

Location
Cottastrasse 34

Bus
41 (Markuskirche)

Fellbach   C–G19–21

The town of Fellbach, in the administrative district of Rems-Murr, extends northward from the vine-clad foothills of the Schurwald, with the Kappelberg (469 m (1539 ft); nature trail), over the fertile Schmidener Feld, an area of ancient settlement. With the districts of Schmiden and Oeffingen, once independent towns, it forms a continuous built-up area between Stuttgart and the Neckar Valley in the west and the Rems Valley in the east.
Originally an agricultural town, its major activity being vine-growing, Fellbach gained its municipal charter in 1933. After

Information
Stadtverwaltung,
G.-Hauptmann-Strasse 17,
7012 Fellbach,
tel. 5 85 13 61

S-Bahn
S 2, 3 (Fellbach)

Buses
60, 7930, 7932 (Fellbach)

Fellbach

Tram
1 (Fellbach)

Distance
8 km (5 miles) north-east as
the crow flies

the Second World War it enjoyed a great economic upsurge,
following the establishment here of many prominent industrial
firms (Herion, Lechler, Wega, etc.). With a population of only
15,000 in 1939, the town has now a population, including the
districts of Schmiden and Oeffingen, of well over 40,000.

Jugendhaus

Location
Esslinger Strasse 100

The Jugendhaus (Youth House), on the western outskirts of
Fellbach, is perhaps the most interesting building of the kind in
the Stuttgart area. Designed by the Innsbruck architect J.
Lackner, it shows a well-contrived articulation of the interior
designed to meet the needs of its users. The central feature is a
spiral staircase supporting a glass dome.

Lutheran Church

Location
Hintere Strasse 1

The church, in the oldest part of the town, was surrounded in
the 14th c. by a defensive wall and moat, which were removed
in the 19th c. The sacristy with its reticulated vaulting, the choir
and the tower are Late Gothic. The tower is particularly
attractive with its saddle roof and crowstep gables.

Fellbacher Herbst

The Fellbacher Herbst (Fellbach Autumn) is a wine and harvest
thanksgiving festival held annually and on the second week-
end in October attrating wine-lovers from far and near.

Maria Regina Church   D21

Location
Rembrandtweg 1

The Roman Catholic Parish Church of Maria Regina, on the
east side of the town, was designed by the Stuttgart architect
K. Franz. Elliptical in plan, it is in the form of a truncated cone
with an inclined axis.

*Schwabenlandhalle   E20

Location
Tainer Strasse 7

The Schwabenlandhalle (Swabia Hall), an imposing polygonal
structure of exposed concrete, was designed by G. and W.
Keller and completed in 1976. Well planned to serve a variety
of purposes, it rapidly became one of the leading cultural and
congress centres in the Middle Neckar Valley. It is the scene not
only of musical events and dramatic performances but also of
brilliant balls.

Municipal Museum

Location
Hintere Gasse 26

Opening times
Wed. and Sat. 2–6 p.m., Sun.
10 a.m.–12 noon.

The well-stocked Municipal Museum (Stadtmuseum) displays
a varied range of material of local interest, from fossils to
mementoes and records of old Fellbach families. Its showpiece
is the Schmiden Stag, from a spring sanctuary of the late La
Tène period (Iron Age), the discovery of which some years ago
was a considerable archaeological sensation.

Fellbach Triennale

This exhibition of small sculptures, first held in summer 1980, has aroused great interest. The work is mainly by German artists.

Vine-Growers' Co-operative

The Fellbach Vine-Growers' Co-operative (Weingärtner-genossenschaft), founded in 1857, now has 310 members with 170 hectares (420 acres) of vineyards on the Kappelberg. The vineyard names are Weinsteige, Wetzstein (Riesling), Goldberg, Hinterer Berg and Lämmler (which is particularly renowned).

Visits and tastings by appointment (tel. 58 78 61)

Feuerbach
D–F9–11

Feuerbach, now a district of Stuttgart with extensive industrial installations, first appears in the records in 1075 under the name of Biberbach. A cemetery of burials arranged in rows above the west side of the old town centre points to the existence of a settlement of the Merovingian period. During the Middle Ages there was a castle here, some remains of which were recently excavated. The town gained its municipal charter in 1907. Its rapid industrial development and growth in population were promoted by the coming of the railway in 1846. In the early years of this century the town's prosperity was reflected in the building of houses notable for their variety of architectural form and the elaborate decoration of their façades, such as are still to be seen in the neighbourhood of the Festhalle (by Paul Bonatz; recently renovated) in Steiermärker Strasse (B 295).

S-Bahn
S 4–6 (Feuerbach)

Bus
91

Trams
6, 13

Fire Service Museum (Feuerwehrmuseum)
K13

The Stuttgart Fire Service Museum, housed in No. 1 (South) Fire Station, displays historic old appliances and equipment, including a collection of firemen's helmets ranging from an early leather helmet to the current model made of light metal, fire-alarms, water-buckets and hoses (among them an 18th c. wood pipe and a section of a wood pipeline of about 1700).
Opening times: By appointment (tel. 0711/50 66–2 14)

Location
Heusteigstrasse 12

Bus
41 (Wilhelmstrasse)

Forest Cemetery (Waldfriedhof)
M/N9/10

This beautiful cemetery, situated on the south-western edge of the Stuttgart Basin, was opened in 1914. Among those buried here are Theodor Heuss, first President of the Federal Republic; the great industrialist Robert Bosch; the architect Paul Bonatz; the painter Oskar Schlemmer; Arnulf Klett, first Chief Burgomaster of Stuttgart after the Second World War; the singer Sigrid Onegin, the actor Erich Ponto and the actress Edith Heerdegen.
The memorial to the dead of the First World War was erected in 1929.

Location
Eugen-Dolmetsch-Strasse

Bus
87

Trams
1, 14 (Südheimer Platz, then funicular)

Frauenkopf

Bus
64 (Frauenkopf)

Tram
15 (Stelle)

Distance
3 km (2 miles) south-east

The Frauenkopf (named after a Lady Chapel which once stood here) is a residual hill of Lower Jurassic rock which forms the south-eastern rim of the Stuttgart Basin. On its wooded summit rises the Telecommunications Tower (Fernmeldeturm, 1972), the second highest reinforced concrete tower in Stuttgart (193 m (633 ft)).
On the south-eastern slopes of the hill, which is a popular place of recreation for the people of Stuttgart, lies a residential area, now much sought after, the origins of which go back to the turn of the century.
Lower down are remains of the medieval Castle of Rohreck. On the saddle between the Frauenkopf and the Hoher Bopser, near the Stelle tram stop, is the spot where in 1780 Schiller (see Notable Personalities) read his play "Die Räuber" ("The Robbers") to some of his schoolfellows.

* Fruchtkasten J12(S20)

Location
Schillerplatz 1

U-Bahn
Schlossplatz

Buses
42, 44 (Schlossplatz)

Trams
5, 6, 15 (Schlossplatz)

The Fruchtkasten (Fruit Chest: i.e. Granary) at the south-west corner of Schillerplatz is a Late Gothic stone building with pointed gables (restored in 1954–56), first mentioned in the records in 1393. When Schillerplatz (see entry) was laid out in 1596 it was remodelled by Heinrich Schickhardt in German Renaissance style.
It is planned to use this handsome building to house a museum of contemporary applied art and design.

Funicular (Standseilbahn) M9/10

Trams
1, 14 (Südheimer Platz)

Stuttgart's funicular, opened in 1929, runs up from Südheimer Platz in the district of Heslach to the Forest Cemetery (Waldfriedhof; see entry), 90 m (295 ft) above the square. Its two cars, on an oblique chassis matching the slope of the hill, are linked by a cable which enables one to counterbalance the other as they ascend and descend the 530 m (580 yd) long track, with a gradient of up to 27 per cent.

* German Agricultural Museum S15
(Deutsches Landwirtschaftsmuseum)

Location
Garbenstrasse 9A

Bus
70 (Hohenheim)

Tram
3 (Garbe)

Opening times
Wed., Fri., Sat. and Sun.
10 a.m.–5 p.m. and by appointment

The German Agricultural Museum (opened in 1975), on the campus of Hohenheim University (see entry) offers an excellent survey of the development of agriculture since Neolithic times. The exhibits include the manual implements used by peasant farmers and the various types of machinery which lighten work on the land, documentation on the development of agricultural production and processing techniques, and material illustrating the newer problems of agriculture. Of particular interest are the museum's collection of ploughs (including a gold plough of 1843 and a steam plough of 1920), a collection of implements and appliances made in the old Hohenheim implement factory (including a mowing machine of 1831) and a series of motor tractors.

*German Playing-Card Museum (Deutsches Spielkartenmuseum) T10

The Playing-Card Museum of the Altenburg-Stralsund Company of playing-card manufacturers, which has been in Leinfelden since the end of the Second World War, was established some ten years ago and has recently become a branch of the Württemberg Museum (see entry). In addition to material from the old German Playing-Card Museum in Bielefeld the museum has collections of great artistic and historical interest, including the famous Donndorf luxury cards. Also of interest are the display of fortune-telling cards and the periodic special exhibitions.

Location
Grundschüle Süd,
Schönbuchstrasse 32,
7022 Leinfelden-
Echterdingen

Tram
6 (Leinfelden, Bosch)

Opening times
Tues.–Fri. 2–5 p.m.,
Sun. 10 a.m.–1 p.m.

Geroksruhe K14

The viewpoint of Geroksruhe (417 m (1,368 ft)), on the hillside to the east of Stuttgart, below the Frauenkopf (see entry), is named after the poet and Court Preacher Karl von Gerok (see Notable Personalities). The hill, with footpaths for walkers, affords magnificent views over the Neckar Valley, extending as far as the Löwenstein Hills.

Location
Jahnstrasse

Tram
15 (Geroksruhe)

Glemswald H–P1–7

The Glemswald, a range of Triassic hills formerly clad with forests of oak and beech, bounds the west side of the Stuttgart Basin. Its highest points are the hill crowned by the Palace of

Buses
92 (Solitude)
85, 93 (Schattengrund)

Golden plough (German Agricultural Museum)

Gustav Siegle House

Distance 6 km (4 miles) south-west	Solitude (see entry) and the Bernhartshöne (549 m (1,801 ft)), the highest eminence in the Stuttgart district. The upper course of the Glems stream has been dammed, creating a chain of lakes (see Bärensee, Bärenschlössle). The stream has exposed large outcrops of sandstone. This wooded area, once highly rated as hunting country and still largely intact, offers a varied range of facilities for sport and recreation, for example at the Katzenbacher Hof (see entry).

Solitude Racing Circuit   L–N1–5

Location Schattenring, Glemseck **Buses** 85, 93 (Schattenring)	From 1928 to 1965 the Glemswald was the scene of great events in the motor-racing calendar, when international car and motor-cycle racing stars competed with one another on the Solitude circuit, between the Schattenring and the motorway, which had been specially designed for the purpose. Anything up to 300,000 fans came to watch their idols negotiating the treacherous bends and difficult gradients of the circuit.

Gustav Siegle House   K13(T20)

Location Leonhardsplatz 28 **Buses** 41, 42, 43, 44, 84, 85, 87, 92, 93 (Rathaus) **Trams** 1, 2, 4 (Rathaus)	Gustav Siegle House, designed by Theodor Fischer, founder of the Stuttgart school of architects, and completed in 1912, is an imposing Jugendstil (Art Nouveau) building erected to commemorate Gustav Siegle (1840–1905), a leading industrialist and for many years a member of the Reichstag, by his widow Julie Siegle. The building was badly damaged during the Second World War and was rebuilt by Martin Elsaesser, a pupil of Fischer, in 1953–54. It now belongs to the city of Stuttgart and, in accordance with Julie Siegle's will, is used for various cultural purposes. The main hall (950 seats) and three smaller halls (with a total of 430 seats) provide accommodation for a variety of cultural events (concerts, lectures, etc.). The Stuttgart Antiques Fair is also held here. Notable features of the interior are a bust of Gustav Siegle by Adolf Donndorf the Elder and a mosaic by Professor Gollwitzer. Gustav Siegle House is also the home of the Stuttgart Music School.

*Hanns Martin Schleyer Hall   G16/17

Location Mercedesstrasse 69 **S-Bahn** S 1 (Neckarstadion) **Bus** 56 (Neckarstadion) **Trams** 1, 2 (Mercedesstrasse) 14 (Mineralbader)	The Hanns Martin Schleyer Hall, opened in 1983, was designed to be the last word in European sports stadiums and to accommodate major sporting events, incuding the legendary boxing, handball and athletic contests which previously attracted many thousands of fans to the Killesberg (see entry). The hall has a 285 m (310 yd) cycle-racing track, a removable 200 m (220 yd) circuit for field and track events, special ground surfaces for all kinds of ball games and for dancing competitions and all the necessary facilities for players, the Press, radio and television, as well as administrative and technical services. Up to three 20 m (65 ft) by 40 m (130 ft)

Interior of the Hanns Martin Schleyer Hall

playing areas can be set up at the same time on a temporary basis. There is permanent seating for 5,567 spectators, but if necessary the hall can accommodate 10,471.

The hall, which cost almost 70 million DM, is named after Hanns Martin Schleyer, a Director of Daimler-Benz, President of the German Employers' Federation and President of the Confederation of German Industry, who was murdered by terrorists in October 1977.

Hegel's Birthplace   K12(T19)

The philosopher Georg Wilhelm Friedrich Hegel (see Notable Personalities) was born in ths house on 27 August 1770, the son of Georg Ludwig Hegel, a municipal official, and his wife Maria Magdalena Hegel. In 1776 the family moved to another house in Rödersche Gasse, then a surburban street (now Lange Strasse 7).

Hegel's birthplace was originally a half-timbered house built in the 16th c. and subsequently much altered; the façade is 18th c. On the 200th anniversary of the philosopher's birth the house was thoroughly renovated and opened to the public as a Hegel memorial.

Location
Eberhardstrasse 53

Buses
41, 42, 43, 44, 84, 85, 87, 92, 93, 7945 (Rathaus)

Trams
1, 2, 4 (Rathaus)

Hindenburgbau

See Arnulf-Klett-Platz

Hirschstrasse   J/K12(T19/20)

Bus
43 (Rotebühlplatz)

Trams
2, 4, 14 (Rotebühlplatz)

Hirschstrasse, which runs parallel to Königstrasse from the Marktplatz, is one of the oldest traffic arteries in the town centre. About 1715, when the Nesenbach (later diverted) flowed along the street, it was known as Stadtgasse; it was given its present name in 1740, after a well-known inn (The Stag). It is now a predestrian precinct with excellent small shops.

Hohenasperg

S-Bahn
S 5 (Asperg)

Distance
25 km (15 miles) north

The Hohenasperg (356 m (1,168 ft)), a prominent hill north-west of Ludwigsburg, was already fortified in Celtic times. In the 16th c., during the reign of Duke Ulrich, a castle was built on the hill, defended by strong walls and bastions and a moat. In the 18th c. the castle became a State prison. Among those incarcerated here were Joseph Süss-Oppenheimer, financial adviser to Duke Carl Alexander, the poet and musician Christian Friedrich Daniel Schubart, the economist Friedrich List and the revolutionaries Joseph Fickler and Gottlieb Rau (1848–49). After the Second World War it was used by the Americans as an internment camp. It is now a prison hospital.

*Hohenheim   S/T15/16

Bus
70 (Universität Hohenheim)

Tram
3 (Garbe)

Hohenheim (alt. 391 m (1,283 ft)), situated on the Filder Plateau above the stream of Körsch, south of the city centre, was already the seat of a noble family in medieval times: the name of one Egilolf von Hohenheim appears in the records about 1100. The most celebrated member of the Hohenheim family was the physician and humanist Theophrast Bombast von Hohenheim, better known (from 1529) as Paracelsus – though he spent little time here.

Hohenheim Palace

Hohenheim Castle first appears in the records in 1418, but it was destroyed by fire about 1540. In 1676 the property came into the hands of Emanuel Garb, Jeweller to the Imperial Court, who restored and rebuilt the castle. Then in 1768 Duke Carl Eugen took it over, presenting it four years later to his mistress Franziska von Leutrum (1748–1811), who was created Countess of Hohenheim by the Emperor Joseph II. Carl Eugen spent the last twenty years of his reign with her, marrying her in 1785. During this period the present magnificent palace was built, laid out round a central courtyard and two flanking courtyards.
The main range of buildings, designed by R. F. H. Fischer and erected from 1785 onwards, replaced the medieval moated castle, the foundations of which can still be identified. The main courtyard, the two flanking courtyards and the lateral wings are Baroque, but the elevation shows Neo-classical features – reflecting the new conceptions of Nikolaus Thouret, the Court Architect, who completed the palace (1796 onwards).

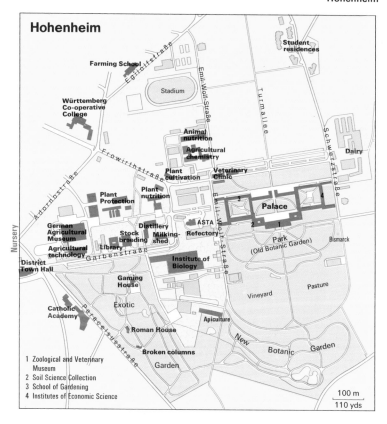

Hohenheim

Farming School

Württemberg Co-operative College

Stadium

Student residences

Emil-Wolf-Straße

Egilolfstraße

Turmallee

Schwarzstraße

Animal nutrition

Agricultural chemistry

Plant cultivation

Veterinary Clinic

Dairy

Frowirthstraße

Adornostraße

Plant Protection

Plant nutrition

m

3

3

1

Palace

4

Nursery

German Agricultural Museum

Agricultural technology

Stock breeding

Library

Distillery

Milking-shed

ASTA

Refectory

2

1

Garbenstraße

District Town Hall

Park (Old Botanic Garden)

Bismarck

Institute of Biology

Gaming House

Pasture

Exotic

Catholic Academy

Paracelsusstraße

Roman House

Apiculture

Vineyard

Broken columns

Garden

New

Botanic

Garden

1 Zoological and Veterinary Museum
2 Soil Science Collection
3 School of Gardening
4 Institutes of Economic Science

100 m
110 yds

The interior of the palace was reconstructed from 1818 onwards to accommodate the Agricultural College, which became Hohenheim University in 1967. Some years ago the ornamental stucco-work by Anton von Isopi (1785) was carefully restored.

Hohenheim University

Carl Eugen and Franziska von Leutrum devoted much care and effort to the creation of a park in the English style. The basic idea was to set the buildings of a farm amid the ruins of a Roman town; and in pursuit of this idea almost a hundred buildings (baths, temples, grottoes, summer-houses, broken columns, etc.) were erected between 1777 and 1793. Of all this there remain the Gaming House, the ruins of a Roman temple and the Roman Inn.

Hohenheim Park

Museum on the History of Hohenheim   S/T15

Opening times
1 Apr.–31 Oct., Sun. and
pub. hol. 10 a.m.–1 p.m. and
2–5 p.m.
1 Nov.–31 Mar., Sun. and
pub. hol. 10 a.m.–1 p.m. and
2–5 p.m.

This little museum, in the Gaming House, contains interesting models of the English Park (made in the time of Carl Eugen) and of the palace in its present state (made by the University Architects' Department), documents on the history of Hohenheim and full documentation on the life of Franziska von Hohenheim, Duke Carl Eugen's mistress and later his wife.
The development of the Agricultural College and the University is illustrated by pictures and records. The exhibits include a portrait of Margarete von Wrangell, the first woman to hold a teaching post in a German institute of higher education.

Economic Archives of Baden-Württemberg   S16

Conducted tours
By arrangement

The Economic Archives (Wirtschaftsarchiv) of Baden-Württemberg, which have been housed since 1981 in the east wing of the palace, contain a collection of old company records (balance-sheets, prospectuses, wages registers, charters, patents, photographs, etc.) which throw light on the economic, and in particular the industrial, development of Baden-Württemberg. The collection, which is being expanded with great vigour, includes extensive records of firms – some still prominent – in the Middle Neckar region, the heartland of Baden-Württemberg's industrial development. Among them are the Werner & Pfeiderer Company of Feuerbach, the Württembergische Metallfabrik of Geislingen and the Boehringer engineering firm of Göppingen.

*Zoological and Veterinary Museum   S15

Opening times
Wed. 10 a.m.–2 p.m.,
Sun. 10 a.m.–4 p.m.

The Zoological and Veterinary Museum (Zoologisches und Tiermedizinisches Museum) is housed in the central block of the palace.
The zoological collections originated in a 19th c. collection devoted to agriculture and forestry.
Exhibits: the lower invertebrates; insects; molluscs, Tentaculata, echinoderms; fishes, amphibians, reptiles; anatomy of the vertebrates; birds; nervous systems; embryology; mammals and man; malformations.
The collection of the Institute of Veterinary Medicine consists mainly of material from the collections of the Stuttgart Veterinary College, which was closed in 1912.
Exhibits: specimens preserved in alcohol; skeletons and individual bones; specimens of historical interest; animals' teeth; historic veterinary instruments; horseshoes, etc.; dogs' pelvises and heads; domestic forms of animals.

Collections of the Institute of Soil Science and Habitat Study   S15

The collections of the Institute of Soil Science and Habitat Study (Institut für Bodenkunde und Standortlehre), housed in the central block of the palace, comprise a geological and palaeontological collection (important index fossils; material from southern Germany), a mineralogical and petrographic collection which includes most of the rock-forming minerals (specimens from the Black Forest and the Alps) and a soil

Hohenheim Palace

Roman House, in the Exotic Garden

science collection, including four sample soil profiles (Hohenheim area; Albrand, near Reutlingen; the Wurzacher Ried; the Rheinaue, near Rastatt).

*Collections of the Institute of Botany   S15

The origins of these collections date back to the foundation of Hohenheim Agricultural College. They offer a systematic presentation of botany (herbaria, glasshouses, botanic gardens). There are notable collections of the vascular plants and fungi of Württemberg in the 19th c. which give valuable information on changes in ecological conditions and damage to the environment which has taken place since then. There is also a very interesting collection of fruits and seeds which is constantly being increased, with special reference to the history of cultivated plants and the history of the flora of Central Europe.

Wood collection

Of special importance is the collection of several thousand specimens of the most important European species of timber, based on an 18th c. collection and covering, with practically no gaps, the last 850 to 900 years.

Agricultural Museum

See German Agricultural Museum

*Old Botanic Garden   S15/126

The Old Botanic Garden occupies the old park, with an area of just under 5 hectares (12½ acres). From 1829 it was planted with a variety of tree species. In front of the west wing of the palace is an avenue consisting mainly of North American conifers. In front of the east wing are old-established deciduous trees, including a mighty hazel tree, a Montpelier maple and various species of magnolia.

The eastern half of the semicircular strip of woodland at the south end of the park contains beautiful Central European and North American deciduous trees, including the sugar maple, the autumn colouring of which is one of the finest sights in the Hohenheim gardens.

*Exotic Garden   S/T15

The Exotic Garden or Arboretum has been cultivated since 1920. It contains well over 1,200 species of trees, including some 230 conifers.

Area 1: North American red oaks, other oaks and poplars.
Area 2: dwarf medlars, cherries, plums.
Area 3: limes, alders, *Hibiscus syriacus*.
Area 4: magnolias, rowans, ornamental apple trees, catalpa, cornel.
Area 5: Shrub Terrace.
Area 6: willows, whitethorn, horse chestnuts.
Area 7: larches, Japanese maple.
Area 8: rhododendrons and rhododendron hybrids.

Area   9: hazel trees, elders, false cypresses.
Area 10: yews, false cypresses.
Area 11: birches, beeches.
Area 12: pines, cedars, snowy mespils; sequoia
Area 13: heaths, junipers, birches.
Area 14: firs, hemlocks, spruces.
Area 15: maple, tulip tree, gingko, Austrian pine.

*New Botanic Garden   S/T15/16

The New Botanic Garden was established some years ago in an area of 10 hectares (25 acres) beyond the vineyard and the pasture. The historical section of the gardens displays in exemplary fashion the development of vegetation, both natural and man-made, over the last 12,000 years: vegetation of the Late Glacial period; moorland vegetation; the post-Glacial development of forests in mountain regions (birches, pines, beeches, firs); degenerated mountain forest; the post-Glacial development of forests in upland regions (sea buckthorn, juniper, beech, oak and hornbeam forest); Neolithic forest clearance, with growth of useful plants; Bronze Age clearance, with useful plants; Iron Age clearance, with useful plants; the development of useful plants since Roman times (planting of fruit and ornamental trees, castle and monastery gardens); secondary vegetation (juniper moorland); herb gardens; plantings for research and teaching.
The systematic section of the gardens seeks to represent, in outdoor plantations, the botanical system of useful plants.

*Hoppenlau Cemetery (Hoppenlau-Friedhof)   H/J11/12(R/S18)

The Hopenlau Cemetery, Stuttgart's oldest survivng cemetery, lies between the Liederhalle and the Linden Museum. It was originally opened in 1626 and extended in the mid 17th c.; no burials have taken place here since 1880. On the occasion of the 1961 Federal Garden Show the cemetery was converted into a cemetery park. It derives its very particular atmosphere from the varied style of the tombs, which represent a great range of different artistic trends.

Particularly notable tombs are those of Gustav Schwab, Christian Friedrich Daniel Schubart, Wilhelm Hauff and Johann Heinrich Dannecker and his family (for all of these, see Notable Personalities). Also of interest are the Jewish cemetery, a number of church bells of the 15th–18th c. at the west end of the cemetery and an exhibition of funerary monuments on the north side.

Location
Rosenbergstrasse/
Holzgartenstrasse

Bus
42 (Rosenbergstrasse/
Seidenstrasse)

Tram
4 (Rosenbergstrasse/
Seidenstrasse)

Hospital Church (Hospitalkirche)   J12(S19)

This aisled hall-church was built between 1471 and 1493 on the site of an earlier Lady Chapel in what was then a newly built suburb on the north-west of the town. Work began in 1473 on the building of a monastic house beside the church, and in 1475 this was given into the hands of the Dominicans. After the Reformation and the conversion of the monastery into a

Location
Hospitalstrasse 20

S-Bahn
S 1–6 (Stadtmitte)

Source: City Horticultural Department

1 C. F. Böhringer
(1791–1867), businessman
2 Johann Friedrich, Freiherr
Cotta von Cottendorf
(1764–1832), bookseller and
publisher, politician (place
of burial unknown)
3 J. H. von Dannecker
(1785–1841), Neo-classical
sculptor
4 J. F. Dieterich (1787–1846),
historical painter
5 C. F. Elben (1754–1829),
founder of "Schwäbischer
Merkur"
6 G. C. E. Etzel (1784–1840),
architect
7 F. F. Faber (1789–1858),
genealogist
8 W. F. von Faber du Faur
(1786–1855), metallurgical
engineer, inventor
9 W. Feuerlein (1781–1850),
first Chief Burgomaster of
Stuttgart
10 R. F. H. Fischer
(1746–1813), architect
11 E. F. Georgii (1757–1830),
President of Upper Court,
the "last Württemberger"
12 G. G. Gutbrod (1791–1861),
Mayor of Stuttgart
13 Wilhelm Hauff (1802–27),
poet, writer, editor
14 Friedrich Haug
(1761–1829), poet, librarian
15 C. C. F. Jäger (1773–1828),

doctor, one of founders of
Katharinenhospital
16 G. von Jäger (1785–1866),
geologist, palaeontologist,
honorary citizen of Stuttgart
17 F. Kauffmann (1803–56),
mathematician, lieder-
writer
18 Karl, Freiherr von Kerner
(1775–1840), general,
minister
19 K. F. von Kielmeyer
(1765–1844), scientist,
professor, honorary citizen
of Stuttgart
20 J. D. G. Memminger
(1773–1840), geographer,
statistician
21 Wolfgang Menzel
(1798–1873), writer, critic,
dramatist
22 J. G. von Müller
(1747–1830), copperplate
engraver
23 J. G. von Pahl (1768–1839),
memoir-writer, chronicler
24 Emilie Pistorius
(1776–1816), Uhland's
mother-in-law
25 Theodor Plieninger
(1756–1840), doctor,
honorary citizen of Stuttgart
26 G. H. Rapp (1761–1832),
businessman, bank director,
writer on art
27 George Reinbeck
(1767–1849), poet,

aesthetician, honorary
citizen of Stuttgart; also his
wife Emilie (1794–1846).
(The poet Lenau frequently
stayed with the Reinbecks
between 1832 and 1844.)
28 F. von Römer (1794–1864),
Prime Minister 1848–49,
President of Chamber of
Representatives, honorary
citizen of Stuttgart
29 P. J. Scheffauer
(1756–1808), sculptor
30 Gottlieb Schick
(1776–1812), painter (place
of burial unknown)
31 Albert Schott (1782–1861),
liberal politician
32 C. F. D. Schubart
(1739–91), poet, publicist
33 Gustav Schwab
(1792–1850), poet,
translator
34 J. D. Sick (1733–1801),
wine merchant; and K. F.
Sick (1780–1837), who did
much to promote the
Cannstatt mineral springs
35 G. C. Storr (1746–1805),
theologian, Court Preacher
36 Eberhard von Wächter
(1762–1852), painter
37 K. L. W. Zanth (1796–1857),
architect
38 Emilie Zumsteeg
(1796–1857), singer,
composer, pianist

hospital the Dominican church became the hospital church. The tower was built between 1729 and 1738. The church was destroyed by bombing in 1944; the tower and choir were rebuilt in 1951–60.

In the choir is a Crucifixion (1501) by Hans Seyffer of Heilbronn. In the south aisle can be seen the Sachsenheim Altar (1489). Other notable features are a number of 16th and 17th c. monuments, a memorial commemorating the Reformation (by J. Brüllman, 1917) and the stained glass.

Bus
43 (Rotebühlplatz)

Trams
2, 4, 14 (Rotebühlplatz)

Institute for Relations with Other Countries
(Institut für Auslandsbeziehungen)

See Old Orphanage

Johanneskirche

See St John's Church

Karlshöhe

See Silberburg Gardens

Karlsplatz   J13(S/T20)

This square, planted with chestnut trees, between the Old Palace and the Old Orphanage (see entries), was laid out in 1778, and takes its name from Duke Carl Eugen (see Notable Personalities).

An obelisk was set up in the square in 1795, an ornamental basin in 1807, and in 1898 an equestrian statue (by Ruemann and Thiersch) of the Emperor Wilhelm I.

On the area of grass in front of the Old Palace is a memorial to the victims of National Socialism (by Elmar Daucher, 1970) consisting of four blocks of black granite.

The Saturday mini-flea-market is held in the square.

U-Bahn
Schlossplatz

Bus
44 (Schlossplatz)

Trams
5, 6, 15 (Schlossplatz)

Katzenbacher Hof   N/O4

The Katzenbacher Hof, 1 km (¾ mile) west of Stuttgart in the Esslinger Spitalwald (Esslingen Hospital Forest), is one of the most popular spots in the Glemswald (see entry) recreation area. Associated with the farm is an old forester's house.

To the north of the Katzenbacher Hof lies the Steinbachsee and to the south-east the Katzenbachsee: two artificial lakes created in 1812 by the construction of dams which are linked by canals with the Bärensee (see entry), Neuer See and Pfaffensee.

Location
Esslinger Spitalwald

Buses
81, 85, 93 (Büsnauer Platz)

The Höhenpark in blossom

*Killesberg   E/F12

Bus
43 (Killesberg/Messe)

The Killesberg (383 m (1,257 ft)), an outlier of the Glemswald Hills, rears up between the city centre and the northern district of Feuerbach. Its eastern slopes were laid out from 1937 onwards, in several stages, as a very beautiful park.

*Höhenpark

Location
Am Kochenhof

Bus
43 (Killesberg/Messe)

The Höhenpark (Hill Park), now covering an area of 44 hectares (110 acres), was laid out on the occasion of the National Garden Show of 1939 under the general direction of Hermann Mattern. The creation of the park involved the movement of several hundred thousand tonnes of earth.
Garden shows were held here in 1950 and 1961, the park being freshly laid out on each occasion. Among the special attractions of the park are the Valley of Roses, a water-lily pond, a flower meadow (at its best in summer), a dahlia garden and a lake terrace. Children are catered for by a chair-lift, a miniature railway, a pony-riding school and a well-equipped playground. There is an open-air stage which is used for reggae and rock concerts and a variety of other events.

Variety Theatre
(Summer Theatre)

The latest attraction is the Variety Theatre (264 seats) installed in the former Country Inn at the north end of the park, in which variety shows take place twice daily from May to October.
A variety of places of retirement and an open-air swimming-pool are among the other attractions offered by this most popular of Stuttgart's parks.

Stuttgart Trade Fair

At the south end of the park are a series of exhibition halls, the first of which were erected in the 1950s, with others added over the years since then. There are now thirteen exhibition halls

Location
Am Kochenhof 16

Höhenpark   Killesberg

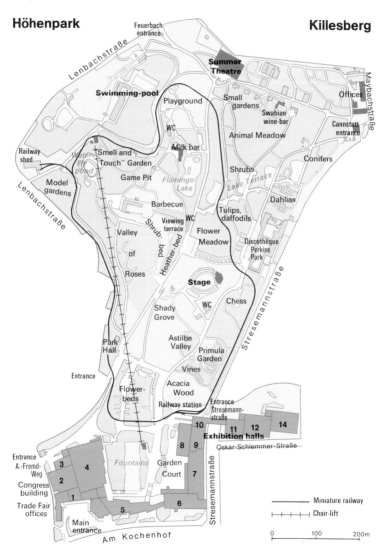

Feuerbach entrance

Lenbachstraße

Summer Theatre

Offices

Maybachstraße

Swimming-pool

Playground

Small gardens

Swabian wine-bar

Cannstatt entrance

WC

Animal Meadow

Railway shed

Milk bar

Water pond

"Smell and Touch" Garden

Shrubs

Conifers

Lenbachstraße

Model gardens

Game Pit

Flamingo Lake

Lake Terrace

Barbecue

Dahlias

Shrub-bed

Viewing terrace

WC

Tulips, daffodils

Valley

Heather-bed

Flower Meadow

Discothèque Perkins Park

of

Roses

Stage

WC

Chess

Stresemannstraße

Shady Grove

Park Hall

Astilbe Valley

Primula Garden

Entrance

Vines

Flower-beds

Acacia Wood

Railway station

Entrance Stresemann-straße

10

11 12 14

Exhibition halls

Oskar-Schlemmer-Straße

8 9

Entrance A.-Fremd-Weg

3

4

Fountains

Garden Court

7

Stresemannstraße

Congress building

2

Trade Fair offices

1

5

6

Main entrance

Am Kochenhof

—— Miniature railway

+—+—+ Chair-lift

0 100 200m

Festival of Light on the Killesberg

Bus
43 (Killesberg/Messe)

(numbered, however, from 1 to 14 – No. 13 being omitted in deference to a superstition shared by many exhibitors) and a congress building. The total floor space available is at present some 40,000 sq. m (48,000 sq. yd). About twenty trade fairs and exhibitions of international standing are held on the Killesberg every year, including such popular events as CMT (International Caravanning, Motoring and Tourism Fair), ISA (International Collectors' Exchange) and Intergastra (an international exhibition of the hotel, restaurant and confectionery trades).

Kleiner Schlossplatz (Little Palace Square)   J12(S19)

U-Bahn
Schlossplatz

Buses
42, 44 (Schlossplatz)

Trams
5, 6, 15 (Schlossplatz)

The Kleiner Schlossplatz occupies the site of the old Kronprinzenpalais (Crown Prince's Palace), destroyed during the last war, which bounded the west side of the Schlossplatz (see entry); a fragment of the palace remains at the descent from the square into Königstrasse. The new square was conceived by the architects, Bächer, Belz and Kammerer, as a "lid" over the elaborate system of underpasses carrying traffic under the square. Surrounded by office buildings and shops, the Kleiner Schlossplatz is broken up by a series of pavilions – the Kartenhäusle (House of Cards), boutiques, cafés, etc. – and offers space for open-air events of the most varied kind.

The square is given a certain atmosphere by a number of pieces of modern sculpture. In front ofthe Mövenpick Restaurant is a work by Herbert O. Hajek.

Below the square, in Königstrasse, is a colourful and much-discussed piece of sculpture, "Crinkly avec disque rouge" (1973) by Alexander Calder (1898–1979), which was purchased by the city in 1980.

Near by are three bronzes by Alfred Hrdlička (born in Vienna, 1929), "Dying Man", "Marsyas I" and "Hommage à Sonny Liston".

It is planned to erect a new Kunstgebäude (Arts Building) in the Kleiner Schlossplatz.

Klett-Passage

See Arnulf-Klett-Platz

*Königsbau   J12(S20)

The Königsbau, which bounds the north-west side of the Schlossplatz (see entry) is an outstanding example of Late Neo-classical architecture, built by Knapp and Leins in 1856–60. The main front facing the square is very characteristic of the Neo-classical school with its two Corinthian porticoes and twenty-six Ionic columns.

Originally designed for social occasions, with ballrooms and concert halls, the Königsbau has been converted to commercial use; but this imposing building nevertheless provides shelter for a variety of hawkers and street musicians.

Location
Schlossplatz

U-Bahn
Schlossplatz

Buses
42, 44 (Schlossplatz)

Trams
5, 6, 15 (Schlossplatz)

*Königstrasse   H/J12/13(R–T19–20)

Königstrasse, for long Stuttgart's finest street and now a pedestrian zone for its whole length, follows the line of the old Grosser Graben (moat), which was filled in and built on during the reign of King Friedrich I of Württemberg, in 1806. It begins at Arnulf-Klett-Platz and the Central Station (see entries), with the tower over the south-eastern entrance hall closing the vista like one of the old town gates. The north-eastern entrance to the street is flanked by the Hindenburgbau, a large department store and, facing this, the Schlossgartenbau, a large commercial complex (Hertie department store, Schlossgarten Hotel, etc.) traversed by three passages.

Farther down the street, opposite the Landesgirokasse (giro bank), is a 3 m (10 ft) high "aquamobile" (fountain). Beyond this, on the left, are St Eberhard's Church (see entry) and, on Schlossplatz (see entry), the Königin-Olga-Bau (Dresdner Bank), built after the last war by Schmitthenner & Partners on the site of the old Danneckerei, the workshop and gallery of antiquities of the sculptor Johann Heinrich Dannecker (see Notable Personalities). Opposite this, on the corner of Bolzstrasse, stands the Marquardtbau (by Eisenlohr and Weigle), opened in 1896 as a high-class hotel and now occupied by shops and offices.

The Schlossplatz, bounded on the right by the Königsbau and the Kleiner Schlossplatz (see entries), divides Königstrasse into a lower and an upper section. The upper section is flanked on both sides by large commercial buildings housing quality shops. The imposing façades and resounding names contribute

U-Bahn
Hauptbahnhof (Arnulf-Klett-Platz), Schlossplatz

S-Bahn
S 1–6 (Hauptbahnhof, Stadtmitte)

Buses
A, 40, 42, 43 (Hauptbahnhof/Arnulf-Klett-Platz)
44 (Schlossplatz)
42, 43 (Wilhelmsbau)

Trams
5, 6, 9, 14, 15 (Hauptbahnhof/Arnulf-Klett-Platz)
5, 6, 15 (Schlossplatz)
2, 4, 14 (Rotebühlplatz)

The Königsbau; in front, the Jubilee Column

Königstrasse, with the Central Station Tower

to the metropolitan character of this part of Königstrasse: e.g. the Salamander-Haus (No. 19A), the Neo-classical building of 1838 (No. 44; now occupied by the Motorways Office), the Bally-Haus (1966; No. 21), the Hertie department store (1946; No. 27), opposite the end of Schulstrasse, and the Mittnacht-bau (No. 46), a reinforced-concrete building faced with travertine (Eisenlohr and Partners, 1926–28), named after a former Prime Minister, Hermann Freiherr von Mittnacht (1825–1909). In the centre of the street can be seen a fine piece of relief sculpture by Dietrich E. Böhm, a figure of a woman. The terminal point of Königstrasse is the Wilhelmsbau with its massive tower (1900), recently renovated at great expense.

Behind the Wilhelmsbau, in Kleine Königstrasse, which links Tübinger Strasse and Marienstrasse, stands the Old Theatre (Altes Schauspielhaus) of 1909, restored and renovated some years ago and now used for productions by visiting companies and as an alternative to the Württemberg State Theatre (see entry).

*Kunstgebäude (Arts Building)   J13(S20)

The Kunstgebäude, the dome of which is topped by a gilded figure of a stag, is a prominent Stuttgart landmark; it was built by Theodor Fischer in 1910–13 on a site once occupied by the Neues Lusthaus, a masterpiece of German Renaissance architecture. Popularly called 'Zum Goldenen Hirsch' (The Golden Stag), it was badly damaged during the Second World War and rebuilt (by Paul Bonatz and Günther Wilhelm) in 1956–61.

In 1920, after the Kapp Putsch, the German Government found a temporary home in the Kunstgebäude.

In front of the Schlossplatz entrance is a fine piece of sculpture by Maillol, "Night" (1909). In addition to the City Gallery the Kunstgebäude also houses exhibitions organised by the Württemberg Art Union (Kunstverein). The Antiques Fair is held here annually in January.

Location
Schlossplatz 2

U-Bahn
Schlossplatz

S-Bahn
S 1–6 (Hauptbahnhof)

Buses
42, 44 (Schlossplatz)

Trams
5, 6, 15 (Schlossplatz)

*City Gallery   J13(S20)

The City Gallery (Galerie der Stadt Stuttgart), originally opened in 1925 as the City Picture Collection (Städtische Gemälde-sammlung) in the Villa Berg (see entry), has been housed in the Kunstgebäude since 1961. The collection extends from the early 19th c. to the present day and consists mainly of the works of South German artists. By concentrating on particular fields, such as the work of Otto Dix, this relatively new gallery has gained a considerable reputation, not confined to specialists.

Arrangement of the collection:

Special exhibitions

Neo-classicism, the Romantic school, Realism and Im-pressionism
Notable works:
Faber du Faur, "Arab with Flag"
Hetsch, "Frau Friederike Rapp with her Child"
Mayer, "Neckar Valley at Berg"

Location
Schlossplatz 2

Opening times
Tues. and Thurs.–Sun.
10 a.m.–5 p.m.,
Wed. 10 a.m.–7 p.m.

Room 1

Rooms 2 and 3

Kunstgebäude

Dome of the Kunstgebäude

	Pilgram, "View of Stuttgart" Schönleber, "Venice" Steinkopf, "River Scene with Horses"
Rooms 4 and 5	Otto Dix Collection Notable works: "The City" (triptych) "Portrait of the Actor Heinrich George" "War" (a series of etchings) "Prager Strasse" "Still Life in the Studio" "Self-Portrait as a Soldier"
Room 6	Sculpture
Rooms 7 and 7A	Adolf Hoelzel and his circle Notable works: Hoelzel, "Mountain Landscape" Baumeister, "Eidos with Landscape" Kerkovius, "Self-Portrait" Schlemmer, "Entrance to the Stadium"
Rooms 8, 9 and 10	Contemporary painting and sculpture Notable works: Böhringer, "Sawmill" Grieshaber, "African Passion" Kokoschka, "Stuttgart"

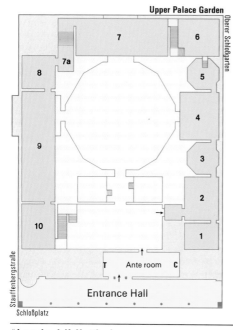

Upper Palace Garden

Oberer Schloßgarten

7

7a

8

6

5

9

4

3

2

1

10

→

T   Ante room   C

↑
← ↑ →

Entrance Hall

Stauffenbergstraße

Schloßplatz

Kunstgebäude

Stuttgart City Gallery

GROUND FLOOR

Permanent collection

1 Special exhibitions
2 Neo-classicism, Romantic school, Realism, Impressionism
3 Impressionism
4,5 Otto Dix Collection
6 Sculpture

UPPER FLOOR
7,7A Adolf Hoelzel and his circle (Baumeister, Schlemmer, Itten, Kerkovius, etc.)
8,9,10 Contemporary painting and sculpture

T Tickets and catalogues
C Cloakroom

Rooms for special events

*Landesbibliothek

See Württemberg Library

Landesbildstelle

See Württemberg Photographic Archives

Landesgewerbeamt   J12(S19)

This monumental domed building was erected in 1889–96 by the Hamburg architect S. Neckelmann to house the Landes-gewerbeamt (Provincial Inspectorate of Factories). It has rich sculptural decoration both externally (portrait medallions of famous Württembergers, coats of arms) and internally. Occupied before the last war by the Industrial Museum, it was badly damaged during the war.
The Landesgewerbeamt now houses the Design Centre (see below); the AV (Audiovisual) Forum, which provides a survey of the development of audiovisual educational aids and offers the services of a "media library"; a library on vocational training; a repository of patents and standard specifications (over 1·7 million patent specifications, some 4 million

Location
Kienestrasse 18

U-Bahn
Universität

Trams
9, 14 (Universität)

Opening times
Mon.–Fri. 9 a.m.–3.30 p.m.

67

Landtag

Landesgewerbeamt

The Landtag building

Design Centre

extracts); an industrial information and documentation centre; the Chemical and Technical Testing Office; and a fashion school which has produced many well-known designers.

The White Hall and Red Hall are occupied by the Design Centre, which displays industrial products selected for the quality of their design and well-made examples of applied art.

Book Weeks

The Stuttgart Book Weeks (Stuttgarter Buchwochen), held here just before Christmas, attract large numbers of visitors to their displays illustrating the range and variety of books published, mainly by publishers in Baden-Württemberg.

Landtag J13(S20/21)

Location
Konrad-Adenauer-Strasse 3

U-Bahn
Charlottenplatz

S-Bahn
S 1–6 (Hauptbahnhof)

Buses
41–44, 73–77, 7600
(Charlottenplatz)

Trams
1, 2, 4, 5, 6, 15
(Charlottenplatz)

The Landtag building, seat of the legislative assembly of Baden-Württemberg, was built in 1955–56 to the design of Kurt Viertel as modified by Erwin Heinle and Horst Linde. A three-storey building on a square plan, it achieves considerable architectural effect with its reinforced-concrete structure, faced with bronze, which is borne on piers on the ground floor. The façade is given further emphasis by its use of dark-toned insulating glass.

The lobby has a fine fossil wall of Lower Jurassic stone from Holzmaden and portraits of prominent Baden-Württemberg politicians. Above the lobby is the main Chamber, surrounded by conference rooms and rooms for members.

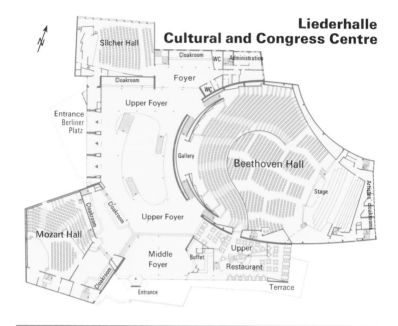

Liederhalle
Cultural and Congress Centre

Lapidarium

See Roman Lapidarium in Old Palace
See Municipal Lapidarium

Leuze-Bad

See Spa establishments (Practical Information)
See Mineral springs

* Liederhalle (Cultural and Congress Centre)   J12(S18)

The Liederhalle was built in 1955–56 to the design of Adolf Abel, Rolf Gutbrod and Blasius Spreng, replacing an earlier hall built by Christian Leins in 1864 for the Stuttgart Choral Society (Liederkranz) which was destroyed by bombing in 1943. The building – now much used as a cultural and communications centre – is given a distinctive appearance by its massive concrete walls, partly faced with quartzite.

Three halls of different sizes, linked by a two-level foyer, provide facilities for a wide range of musical and other occasions – symphony concerts, appearances by visiting stars, congresses, and also lively balls and major fashion shows.

Location
Berliner Platz 1

S-Bahn
S 1–6 (Stadtmitte)

Buses
41, 43 (Berliner Platz/ Liederhalle)

Trams
2, 4, 9, 14 (Berliner Platz/ Liederhalle)

The Beethoven Hall is the largest of the three, with seating for a maximum of 2,019 spectators. It has excellent acoustics and offers good visibility. Interesting features from the architectural point of view are its ground-plan in the form of a grand piano and its elegantly curving gallery.

The Mozart Hall (752 seats) is pentagonal in plan, with the seating arranged in fan shape. The walls are faced with fine woods. Here, too, the acoustics are excellent, being particularly suitable for solo recitals.

The smallest of the three halls, the Silcher Hall (320 seats), is given its particular accent by a wall of glass bricks. In the near future it is planned to build an additional congress building and a hotel complex on to the Liederhalle.

In the Seiden Gardens outside the Liederhalle (corner of Schloss-strasse and Berliner Platz) is a monument (by P. O. Heim) to Philipp Matthäeus Hahn (1739–90), a Swabian pastor and engineer celebrated not only as one of the leading representatives of the Pietist movement in Swabia but also as the initiator of the precision engineering industry in Württemberg.

Linden Museum (State Museum of Ethnology) H12(R18)

Location
Hegelplatz 1

Buses
40, 42, 43 (Hegelplatz)

Opening times
Tues.–Sun. 10 a.m.–5 p.m.,
Thurs. 10 a.m.–8 p.m.

The origins of the Linden Museum, recently reopened after comprehensive repair and restoration, go back to an initiative of the Württemberg Association of Commercial Geography after its foundation in 1882. Under its then President, Count Karl von Linden, the collection of material of ethnographical interest was intensified, and the first fruits of this activity were displayed in the Municipal Industrial Hall by 1885.

Karl von Linden subsequently carried through a plan for building a special Museum of Ethnology, and this was completed in 1911 (architect, Georg Eser).

The museum was badly damaged during the last war, but rebuilding was largely completed by 1950, and in that year the first exhibition of ethnographic material was opened. The reputation of the museum extends far beyond the bounds of the Federal Republic; it is now subsidised by the city of Stuttgart and the *Land* of Baden-Württemberg.

The museum's collections are geographically arranged:

Africa

Reconstruction of a hut selling textiles, souvenirs and contemporary art (north-west Cameroun); façade of a mud hut (northern Nigeria), with a market scene (everyday utensils and implements, textiles, a magnificent decorated saddle); reconstruction of an altar from Benin (Nigeria), with bronze and ivory objects; craft articles from the steppe and coastal regions; façade from a house in the primeval forest (Cross River area, Cameroun), with masks and cult figures from eastern Nigeria and western Cameroun; reconstruction of the entrance to a palace; masks from the Cameroun grasslands; craft objects from Gabon, Zaire and East Africa.

North America

Prairie and plain areas, with older (1830s) and recent material (period of reservations); reconstruction of a Mandan house; Pueblo Indians and southern Athabaskans (Apaches and Navahos); California, continuing up the north-west coast to Alaska; the Eskimos.

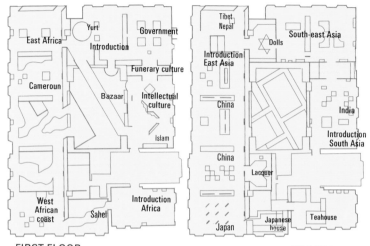

FIRST FLOOR
Africa, Orient

SECOND FLOOR
East Asia, South Asia

Linden Museum
State Museum of Ethnology

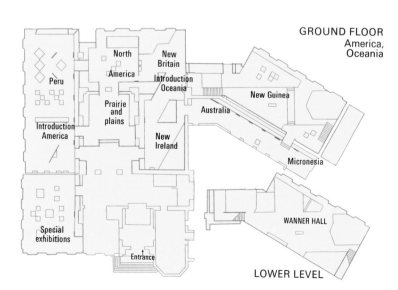

GROUND FLOOR
America,
Oceania

LOWER LEVEL

Linden Museum: Indian bison robe (detail)

The exhibits consist mainly of clothing, weapons, domestic equipment and craft objects.

Pre-Columbian Peru

Early origins: Chavin, early Mochica and Recuay, and south coast (Paracas). Classic period: mainly Mochica and Recuay, Nazca. Late period: Huari, Chimu, Chancay, the Incas.
Mainly pottery and textiles, with some woodcarving and metalwork.

Australia

Cultures of the Aboriginals of central Australia: everyday and ceremonial equipment.

Melanesia

Bismarck Archipelago (cultures of New Ireland, New Britain and Manus): masks, sculpture, everyday objects.
Sepik region: conceptions of creation, initiation, head-hunting, ancestor worship; reconstructions of a ceremonial house and an initiation hut.

Micronesia

Culture of Palau

Islamic section

Religion: the Koran, mosque furnishings, tombs of holy men, popular religious feeling.
Science: astronomy, medicine.
Books and calligraphy.
The Islamic town; life of the higher social classes in the medieval period.
Government and State; furnishings of a palace.
Reconstruction of a street in the Tashkurgan bazaar.
A Turkoman yurt, furnished, as an example of rural nomadic life-style.

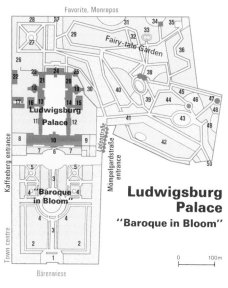

1 Main entrance	28 Aviaries
2 Rose-gardens	29 Flamingo Meadow
3 Fountain Avenue	30 Aviaries
4 Display of rose varieties	31 Playground
	32 Water Garden
5 Baroque gardens	33 Gondola Pond
6 Spring flowers	34 Herzogschaukel
7 Dahlias	(Duke's Swing)
8 Friedrichsgarten	35 Puppet Theatre
9 Queen's Garden	36 Information Garden
10 New Corps de Logis	37 Favorite entrance
11 Picture Gallery	38 Emichsburg
12 Ancestors' Gallery	39 Rhododendron Valley
13 West wing	40 Valley of Bird Song
14 East wing	41 Spring Flowers Walk
15 Theatre	42 Large Aviary
16 Festinbau	43 Schlüssele-See (fountain)
17 Guard-room	44 Shrubbery
18 Ordenskapelle	45 Garden of Rarities
19 Church	46 Display of summer flowers
20 Riesenbau	47 Vinery
21 Ordensbau	48 Japanese Garden
22 Kitchens	49 Park Café
23 Hunting Pavilion	50 Posilipo entrance
24 Old Corps de Logis	
25 Gaming Pavilion	
26 Baroque and Renaissance gardens	
27 Grosse Broderie (Embroidery)	

Ludwigsburg Palace
"Baroque in Bloom"

*Ludwigsburg

Ludwigsburg (alt. 196–328 m (643–1,076 ft)), a regularly planned town known as the "Swabian Versailles", lies on the Langes Feld Plateau. It is now the chief town of a rural district (*landkreis*) and a considerable industrial and educational centre (teachers' training college). It has a population of some 80,000.

Burials found within the area of the town show that there was a settlement here in the 6th–7th c.

In 1704 work began on the construction of a splendid new palace, named in the following year Ludwigsburg, for Duke Eberhard Ludwig, who ordered the building of the palace to please his mistress Countess Wilhelmine von Graevenitz. The site was close to a former monastic property, the Erlachhof.

Some years later the Duke set about founding a town in the immediate vicinity of the palace. At first he had little success, and it was only after he had held out the prospect of freedom of trade, freedom of religion, two markets and independent administration of justice that the first craftsmen, porters and innkeepers began to settle in the town. The Italian architect Frisoni was soon commissioned to plan the new town, with a Baroque central area the layout and elevations of which are still impressive. The focal point of the town was the market square – one of the finest in Germany – dominated by the Protestant parish church (Stadtkirche) and the Roman Catholic Trinity Church (both 18th c.).

In 1724 Ludwigsburg became the residence and capital of the Duke of Württemberg; but a few years later Duke Carl

Information
Fremdenverkehrsamt, Wilhelmstrasse 12, 7140 Ludwigsburg, tel. 07141/9 10–2 52

S-Bahn
S 4, 5 (Ludwigsburg)

Distance
20 km (12½ miles) north

Ludwigsburg Palace, south front

Alexander moved back to Stuttgart, bringing Ludwigsburg to the verge of ruin. It was only when Duke Carl Eugen returned to Ludwigsburg and held splendid Court there between 1764 and 1775 that the town again enjoyed a brief period of prosperity; but when Carl Eugen moved away again there was a further decline.

At the end of the 18th c. King Friedrich of Württemberg (1797–1816) made Ludwigsburg his summer residence, but after his death Stuttgart again became the sole capital of Württemberg. By way of compensation the largest garrison in the country was stationed in Ludwigsburg. The coming of the railway in 1846 fostered the establishment of industries which were to have a very positive influence on the town's further development.

**Ludwigsburg Palace

S-Bahn
S 4, 5 (Ludwigsburg)

Conducted tours
Apr.–Oct., 9 a.m.–noon and 1–5 p.m.; Nov.–Mar., Mon.–Fri. 10.30 a.m. and 3 p.m., Sat., Sun. and pub. hol. 10.30 a.m., 2 and 3.30 p.m.

Information
Tel. 07141/1 41 24 40

Ludwigsburg Palace is the largest Baroque complex of its kind in Germany. The first part of the palace, now known as the Old Corps de Logis (Altes Corps de Logis), was built in 1704 by P. F. Jenisch in the style of an Italian palazzo. Then in 1707 J. F. Nette began work on the Ordensbau and Riesenbau, two side wings built at right angles to the original building. Seven years later the Fürstenbau, with galleries and corner pavilions, was added.

In 1714 D. G. Frisoni took over the direction of the work, building the church, the Ordenskapelle and the two flanking wings. In 1725 and subsequent years the New Corps de Logis (Neues Corps de Logis) and the garden front were built under the direction of P. Retti. The grand courtyard was now completely enclosed. Thereafter work on the palace continued under Duke Carl Eugen (architects, D. Leger and L. P. de la Guêpière) and King Friedrich I (architect, Nikolaus Thouret). The exterior of the palace displays the Baroque architecture of Italy and eastern Central Europe, reflecting the style of the various architects involved. French influences can also be detected, particularly in the flanking wings and the galleries.

Sumptuously decorated staircases lead up from a beautifully painted vestibule to the main floor, with figures by the Italian artist Diego Carlone. In the Guard-room (Gardesaal) the influence of the Neo-classical architect Nikolaus Thouret can be seen. The marble figures of women bearing torches are by J. H. Dannecker. The Marble Hall (Marmorsaal) and the Ducal apartments are also Neo-classical in style.

New Corps de Logis
(Neues Corps de Logis)

This museum, on the upper floor, is a branch of the Württemberg Museum (see entry). It displays fine 18th c. furniture and furnishings, reflecting the taste of Duke Carl Eugen in particular.

Museum of Baroque Courtly Art (Museum "Höfische Kunst des Barock")

The house was decorated about 1810 to Thouret's design. The stage machinery of 1759 is well preserved.

Theatre
(Schlosstheater)

The church is domed, with massive columns supporting the roof. Its principal treasure is the altar-piece by Carlo Carlone, "Institution of the Last Supper". The fresco in the dome is by the same artist. The statues of David and Solomon are by Diego Carlone.

Church
(Hofkirche)

The Riesenbau contains the apartments of the Ducal Prince and the Crown Prince, with an audience chamber (sumptuous Rococo interior) and the Porcelain Cabinet (Ludwigsburg, Meissen, Nymphenburg and Frankenthal porcelain).

Riesenbau
(Giant Building)

The interior of the Gaming Pavilion is perhaps the finest in the whole palace, dating from the first twenty years of the 18th c. The ceiling-fresco, "Allegories of the Seasons", is by E. Wohlhaupter, the stucco-work by Diego Carlone.

Gaming Pavilion
(Spielpavillon)

The Old Corps de Logis contains the apartments of the Crown Princess and the Duke. In the Crown Princess's audience chamber are Brussels tapestries and a ceiling-fresco by Steinfels, "Mars Asleep". In the antechamber of the apartments is another ceiling-painting by Steinfels, "Diana and her Train". The finest room in the Duke's apartments is the Mirror Cabinet (Spiegelkabinett), with valuable Chinese porcelain.

Old Corps de Logis
(Altes Corps de Logis)

The Marble Room (Marmorsaletta) in the Hunting Pavilion has a Rococo interior, with sculpture by Diego Carlone and a riotous ceiling-painting by Colomba, "Apollo". Beyond the Saletta are a Chinese Lacquer Cabinet (Chinesisches Lack-kabinett), a Marble Cabinet (Marmorkabinett) and a Panelled Cabinet (Boiseriekabinett; decoration by J. J. Mayer). The pavilion also houses a display of the products of the Procelain Manufactory (which can be bought here).

Hunting Pavilion
(Jagdpavillon)

In the Ordensbau – the counterpart of the Riesenbau – is the Ordenssaal, in which the constitution of the kingdom of

Ordensbau

Ludwigsburg

Favorite

Monrepos

Württemberg was proclaimed on 25 September 1819 and the republican constitution of the *Land* of Württemberg on 25 September 1919.

The ceiling-fresco of Athena was painted by Scotti and Baroffio in 1731. The staircase has an imposing "Glorification of Hercules".

Ordenskapelle

In the antechamber is a bronze bust of King Friedrich by Dannecker. On the walls are heraldic emblems. The Rococo chapel is one of the finest in south-western Germany, with stucco-work by Brilli, carving by Roger and a ceiling-fresco by L. Retti.

Palace Festival and Concerts

Informatijon
Sekretariat de
Schlossfestspiele,
tel. 07141/2 80 00

The Ludwigsburg Palace Festival, held annually from May to October, and the Ludwigsburg Palace Concerts, during the winter months, have established reputations extending far beyond the bounds of Württemberg.

* Porcelain Manufactory

Opening times
Mon.–Fri. 9.30 a.m.–noon
and 2.30–4.30 p.m.

The renowned Ludwigsburg Porcelain Manufactory, housed in the palace, was established by Duke Carl Eugen in 1756–58. It produces white porcelain based on old designs. There is a showroom and sales point in the Hunting Pavilion.

** "Baroque in Bloom" (Blühendes Barock)

"Baroque in Bloom" (Blühendes Barock) is the name given to the palace gardens, redesigned in 1954 on the basis of 18th c. plans to mark the 250th anniversary of the palace. The beautiful and intricately patterned flower-beds, the basins and fountains re-create the splendour of Court life in the Baroque period. Attractions added in recent years are the Fairy-tale Garden (Märchengarten), the Valley of Bird Song (Tal der Vogelstimmen) and a large aviary. The gardens (30 hectares (75 acres)) form a magnificent backdrop for "festivals of light", concerts and other events.

One of the major events in the annual programme of "Baroque in Bloom" is the Schwäbische Floriade, a display by the Württemberg Horticultural Society.

S-Bahn
S 4, 5 (Ludwigsburg)

Opening times
End Mar.–mid Oct., daily
7.30 a.m.–8.30 p.m.

Conducted tours
By arrangement

* Schloss Favorite

The little palace of Favorite was built for Duke Eberhard Ludwig as a hunting-lodge by Nette, Frisoni and Retti, who completed it in 1723. It is approached by a very handsome staircase leading up to the central pavilion, crowned by towers.

The interior was redecorated in Neo-classical style by Thouret in 1801–04, retaining the original arrangement of the rooms.

In the cellar is a gigantic wine-cask (capacity about 900 hectolitres (20,000 gallons)) of 1720, with fine carving by Seefried.

The Favorite Park is a nature park and deer-park which attracts many visitors. Particularly pleasing is the path linking Schloss Favorite with Schloss Monrepos.

S-Bahn
S 4 (Favoritepark,
Ludwigsburg)

Distance
25 km (15 miles) north

Opening times
Daily 9 a.m.–noon and
1.30–5 p.m.

Favorite Park

* Schloss Monrepos

This little palace, on the shores of a lake, lies to the north-west of the town. Built for Duke Carl Eugen in 1760–66 by L. P. de la Guêpière, it shows the influence of French architecture. The domed central rotunda is approached from the lakeside by a curving staircase.

The interior was altered in Neo-classical style by Nikolaus Thouret for King Friedrich I of Württemberg. The painting in the dome of the rotunda was the work of N. Guibal. Other artists who contributed to the decoration included P. J. Scheffauer and P. Lejeune.

To the west of the palace are the domestic offices, a long procession of buildings also dating from the 18th c.

Attractive boating on the lake. Near by are the Duke of Württemberg's wine-cellars (wine-tasting by appointment) and the Monrepos Hotel.

S-Bahn
S 4 (Favoritepark,
Ludwigsburg)

Distance
23 km (14 miles) north

Opening times
Mar.–Oct., 9–11 a.m. and
3–6 p.m.

Hoheneck Spa (Heilbad Hoheneck)

The old-established spa establishment of Hoheneck, situated high above the Neckar, has been completely modernised in recent years. It now has a brine bath for exercise therapy, a therapeutic products department and a "Mediterraneum" which has become a very popular attraction.

Location
Uferstrasse 50

S-Bahn
S 4 (Favoritepark,
Ludwigsburg)

Opening times
Mon. 10 a.m.–8 p.m., Tues.
and Thurs. 8 a.m.–9 p.m.,
Wed. and Fri. 8 a.m.–8 p.m.,
Sat. and Sun. 8 a.m.–5 p.m.

Treatment at Hoheneck is recommended for rheumatism,
conditions of the joints and spinal column, gynaecological
disorders and disturbances of the automatic nervous system.

*Marbach am Neckar

Information
Stadtverwaltung,
Marktstrasse 23,
7142 Marbach am Neckar,
tel. 07144/1 92 92

S-Bahn
S 4 (Marbach)

Distance
35 km (22 miles) north

The little town of Marbach am Neckar (pop. 12,000), best
known as the birthplace of the great poet and dramatist
Friedrich Schiller (b. 1759), is charmingly situated high above
the right bank of the Neckar. The town first appears in the
records in 972. The old part of the town is very attractive, with
the main street (market) traversing it from east to west. Notable
buildings are Schiller's birthplace (see below), the old Schloss
(end of 17th c.; now a courthouse), the Town Hall (1762) and
the Late Gothic St Alexander's Church (Protestant), an early
work by Aberlin Jörg.

*Schiller's Birthplace

Location
Nicklastorstrasse 31

Opening times
Daily 9 a.m.–noon and
1–6 p.m.

Friedrich Schiller (see Notable Personalities) was born on
10 November 1759 in this modest half-timbered house in
Nicklastorstrasse. The house was renovated and altered by
Leins in 1859, and is now a Schiller memorial, with household
equipment belonging to the Schiller family, contemporary
likenesses of Schiller and a copy of a bust of the poet by
Dannecker.

**National Schiller Museum and German Literary Archives
(Schiller-Nationalmuseum, Deutsches Literaturarchiv)

Location
Schillerhöhe 8–1

Opening times
Museum: daily 9 a.m.–5 p.m.
Archives: Mon.–Fri.
8.30 a.m.–5.30 p.m.

Conducted tours
By arrangement

Information
Tel. 07144/60 61

The National Schiller Museum and the German Literary
Archives associated with it are one of the most famous centres
of literary research in Germany, with manuscripts, printed
books and other documents concerning German literature
available for consultation by scholars and others interested.
The National Schiller Museum (by Eisenlohr and Weigle,
1903), standing high above the banks of the Neckar, is
reminiscent in form of the Palace of Solitude (see entry). It was
considerably enlarged in 1934; the modern building housing
the German Literary Archives was added in 1972 (architects,
E. and J. Kiefner and W. Lauber).
The Schiller Museum, established on the initiative of the
Swabian Schiller Society, was founded in the 19th c. Its further
development was bound up with the personality of Otto von
Güntter, under whose direction it attained international
reputation. During the Second World War the museum's
archives were removed to safe storage, and in 1947 they were
returned to the museum, which had survived the war
unscathed. The collection was considerably enriched when the
"Stuttgarter Zeitung" presented the records of the publishing
firm of Cotta (see Notable Personalities) to the museum. After
the foundation of the German Literary Archives as part of the
museum in 1955, the museum's holdings of archives were
much expanded.

Schiller's birthplace, Marbach ▶

Market Hall

Range of the museum's holdings	Documentation on the life and work of all important German poets and writers from the 18th c. to the present day. The collection is particularly strong in material on Swabian writers including Schiller, Mörike, Hölderlin, Hauff, Kerner and Uhland. Letters, diaries, manuscripts and printed works from the papers left by writers and other collections. Records of publishers; works by German literary exiles; library (over 200,000 volumes); photographic records; recordings; posters; newspaper cuttings; special catalogues; theatre programmes; and numerous other publications and mementoes.
Special exhibitions, etc.	There are frequent special exhibitions, lectures on German literary subjects and readings by authors, organised by the museum.

---

*Market Hall (Markthalle)   J13(S/T20)

Location
Dorotheenstrasse 4

U-Bahn
Schlossplatz

Buses
42, 44 (Schlossplatz)

Trams
5, 6, 15 (Schlossplatz)

The Municipal Market Hall (Städtische Markthalle) is one of Stuttgart's most interesting Jugendstil (Art Nouveau) buildings. It was designed by its architect, Martin Elsaesser, as a combination of a food market and a warehouse; and this concept has proved its worth, as the presence of some sixty dealers (selling flowers, vegetables, exotic fruits, spices, meat and sausages, fish, bakeries, etc.) indicates.

The present Market Hall, with frescoes by Gref and Rümelin on its external walls and arcading giving the exterior its distinctive note, replaces an earlier one established by King Wilhelm I which soon became too small.

Opening times: Mon.–Fri. 10 a.m.–6 p.m., Sat. 7 a.m.–2 or 4 p.m.

Marktplatz (Market Square)   J12/13(T20)

U-Bahn
Rathaus

Buses
41, 42, 43, 44, 84, 85, 87, 92, 93 (Rathaus)

Trams
1, 2, 4 (Rathaus)

The Marktplatz first appears in the records in 1304, and has from time immemorial been a centre of trade and communications. Down the centuries it has been much enlarged. The first Town Hall (see entry), was built in the square in 1456. Known as the "Herrenhaus", it stood here until 1820. It also served as a courthouse, in which the legendary Süss (see Notable Personalities) was condemned to death.

The square suffered heavy damage during the Second World War, but was restored to its position as one of the city's focal points in the 1950s – as the typical post-war façades of the shops and office buildings round the square bear witness.

On the west side of the square is an information column, kept up to date by the city's Press and Information Office.

Market Fountain

In recent years the square has become a pedestrian precinct. One of its features is the Market Fountain (Marktbrunnen), the basin of which is faced with cast-iron panels decorated with allegorical figures, hunting and military scenes, the Württemberg coat of arms and the monogram of Duke Eberhard Ludwig. The panels were cast in Königsbronn, near Heidenheim, in 1713. The central column of the fountain was designed by Nikolaus Thouret.

Market Hall

Market Square

Market Fountain

Schulstrasse	From the north-west side of the Marktplatz a narrow little street, Schulstrasse, leads up to Königstrasse. Its name first appears in the records as early as 1425. It became a pedestrian precinct in the 1950s – the first in the Federal Republic.
Breuninger's	On the south-east side of the square is Breuninger's department store, which celebrated its 100th anniversary some years ago. The store, which has branches in Sindelfingen and Ludwigsburg, is still rated one of the best places to shop in Germany.

Max-Eyth-See (Max Eyth Lake)

Location
Stuttgart-Hofen

Bus
54 (Seeblickweg)

Tram
14 (Max-Eyth-See)

This lake, with an area of 17 hectares (42 acres), was created in 1935 by the damming of the Neckar at Hofen. It is named after the celebrated engineer and writer Max Eyth (1836–1906), constructor of the steam plough. The lake is now the central feature of an excellently equipped recreation park (sailing, wind-surfing, canoeing, rowing, electric boats; bird island; fishing; facilities for games and sunbathing; footpath round the lake, etc.).

Mineral springs (Mineralquellen) F/G14/15

Location
Stuttgart-Bad Cannstatt,
Stuttgart-Berg

Trams
1, 2, 14 (Mineralbäder)

Boat landing-stage
Wilhelma

The most abundant sources of mineral water in western Europe are to be found in and around Bad Cannstatt (see entry), where one natural spring, twenty-three drilled wells and numerous other outlets yield some 300 litres (66 gal) of warm or hot water per second. The most productive sources are in the Kursaal (Wilhelmsbrunnen, Gottlieb-Daimler-Quelle), the spa establishment at Leuze (Inselquelle, Leuzequelle), the Berg spa establishment (five artesian wells), the Untere Anlagen (Hirschquelle, Schwefelquelle) and the grounds of the Cannstatt Schwimmverein.

The Cannstatt springs were already known in Roman times. In the 19th c. they gave the rising spa of Bad Cannstatt a reputation extending far beyond the bounds of Württemberg. Used in the form of the Stuttgart treatment (Stuttgarter Kur) devised some years ago, they have achieved rapid and lasting cures of patients suffering from rheumatism and disorders of the metabolism, cardiac conditions and circulatory troubles.

The Stuttgart waters fall into three different categories:

1 ferrunginous, containing calcium and sodium chloride;

2 acidic, containing sodium and calcium chlorides and sulphates and hydrogen carbonate; and

3 containing calcium and hydrogen carbonates.

Möhringen P–T9–12

Buses
72, 87, 7600

Trams
3, 5, 6

Möhringen, one of Stuttgart's largest wards in terms both of area and population, lies to the south of the city centre in the Filder area, conveniently situated from the point of view of communications, with the motorway and the airport within easy reach.

Fountains in Bad Cannstatt . . .   *. . . and in Berg*

Originally an Alemannic settlement, the place changed masters many times in the course of its history. It was incorporated in Stuttgart in 1942.

The old town centre, with some well-preserved half-timbered buildings, is dominated by St Martin's Church (Protestant), built by Hans Böblinger in 1460–64, enlarged in 1493 and remodelled in Neo-Gothic style in 1852–55.

The Esslinger Spitalhof, a complex of half-timbered buildings in Filderbahnstrasse dating from 1496, was badly damaged during the last war and subsequently pulled down. In 1959–60 part of it was rebuilt, the reconstruction of the gatehouse (1568) being particularly well done. An interesting local museum is now housed here (Filderbahnstrasse 29; open Sat. and Sun. 10 a.m.–noon). Present-day Möhringen is characterised by its industrial buildings. Among them is the Züblin-Haus (by Gottfried Böhm, 1985), which strikes an unusually imposing note.

Fasanenhof   S10/11

This satellite town designed for a population of 8,000, lying to the south of the old village of Möhringen beyond the stream of Körsch, aroused a great deal of interest when it was built in the 1960s. It occupies the site of a pheasantry established by Duke Eberhard Ludwig in 1730: hence the name Fasanenhof (Pheasant Court). The dominant feature of this dormitory suburb is the Salute tower block, designed by the distinguished architect Hans Scharoun.

Bus
72 (Fasanenhof)

Möhringen Printing and Publishing Centre   R12

Location
Plieninger Strasse 100

Buses
73–77, 7600 (Landhaus)

Tram
3 (Landhaus)

The concentration of Press-ownership led to the creation, in the industrial zone south-east of Möhringen, of the Printing and Publishing Centre (Verlags- und Druckzentrum), which began to operate in 1976. This is the new home of the "Stuttgarter Zeitung", the "Stuttgarter Nachrichten" and the "Illustrierte Wochenzeitung", and the plates for many regional papers are also produced here. "Sonntag Aktuell", one of the biggest-circulation Sunday papers in southern Germany, was founded here some years ago.

Mühlhausen

Bus
54

Tram
14

Stuttgart's Mühlhausen ward lies on both banks of the Neckar on the north side of the city. The two old settlements which form its core, Mühlhausen on the left bank and Hofen on the right bank, have a long history. Recently the largest Neolithic cemetery in Germany was found in a field within the ward. The old town of Mühlhausen, long the site of a castle, was particularly famed for St Vitus's Chapel (see entry), a jewel of Gothic architecture.

Also within Mühlhausen ward are two new districts, Freiberg (pop. about 8,000, on left bank of Neckar) and Neugereut (pop. about 6,500, on right bank of Neckar above Hofen), which were developed on green-field sites between 1974 and 1977 and are much admired as examples of modern town-planning.

Municipal Archives

See Wilhelmspalais

Municipal Lapidarium (Städtisches Lapidarium)   K12

Location
Mörikestrasse 24

Bus
41 (Marienstrasse/
Silberburgstrasse)

Opening times
Wed. and Sat. noon–5 p.m.,
Sun. 10 a.m.–noon

The Municipal Lapidarium, housed in an old villa and its gardens, displays architectural elements from famous Stuttgart buildings which have been destroyed or demolished: remains of the Königstor, the Lusthaus and the Old Town Hall, inscriptions, stones bearing coats of arms, sculpture (including originals of works by Dannecker and a reproduction of his group of nymphs), funerary monuments of various periods and a collection of Roman antiquities.

*Neckar Stadium (Neckarstadion)   G17

Location
Mercedesstrasse 71

S-Bahn
S 1 (Neckarstadion)

The Neckar Stadium, Stuttgart's largest sports arena, with accommodation for 70,600 spectators, was built in 1933 (architect, Paul Bonatz) for the German Gymnastics Festival, enlarged for the Gymnastics Festival of 1973 and further improved for the world football championship matches in 1974. The stadium now has 18,000 seats under cover and

The Neckar Stadium

17,600 in the open, together with standing accommodation for 35,000. The playing area measures 68 m (74 yd) by 105 m (115 yd). Surrounding the pitch is a 400 m (440 yd) running-track with eight lanes and all the necessary facilities for field and track events. Under the main stand are six training-halls for fencing, judo, gymnastics, wrestling, table-tennis and dancing. The stadium is equipped with an electronic scoreboard and floodlighting with a power of 1,500 lux. The Nectar Stadium is the home of Stuttgart's football team, VfB.

Adjoining the stadium is the ultra-modern Hanns Martin Schleyer Hall (see entry).

Bus
56 (Neckarstadion)

Trams
1, 14 (Mineralbäder),
2 (Mercedesstrasse)

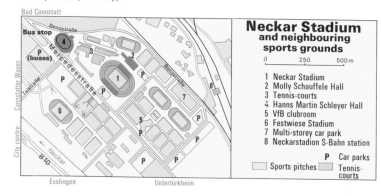

Neckar Stadium
and neighbouring
sports grounds

0   250   500 m

1 Neckar Stadium
2 Molly Schauffele Hall
3 Tennis-courts
4 Hanns Martin Schleyer Hall
5 VfB clubroom
6 Festwiese Stadium
7 Multi-storey car park
8 Neckarstadion S-Bahn station

P Car parks

Sports pitches   Tennis-courts

*Neckar Valley

Location
Obertürkheim,
Untertürkheim, Wangen,
Hedelfingen, Bad Cannstatt,
Münster, Mühlhausen and
Hofen wards

The Neckar flows through the north-eastern and eastern districts of Stuttgart. Between Esslingen and Obertürkheim it leaves the Middle Keuper (Triassic) hills and forms a wide gravel plain, mainly filled with Upper Jurassic detritus. This level area is now occupied as far as Bad Cannstatt by industrial and port installations, with some intervening residential areas. Between Obertürkheim and the district of Münster, which has a large waste – incinerating plant, the river flows between terraces of calc tufa (travertine).

The valley opens out at Cannstatt, and the Neckar then cuts its way into the Middle Triassic limestone, flowing beyond Münster in a narrow enclosed valley. In the large bend at Mühlhausen and Hofen is the Max-Eyth-See (see entry), and artificial lake created by damming the river.

The sunny slopes of the valley in this area produce some of Württemberg's finest wines, such as Cannstatter Zuckerle, which own their high quality, among other factors, to the good limestone soil.

Cruises on the Neckar, starting from the Wilhelma Gardens: see Practical Information.

*New Palace (Neues Schloss)

Location
Schlossplatz

U-Bahn
Schlossplatz

Buses
42, 44 (Schlossplatz)

Trams
5, 6, 15 (Schlossplatz)

In 1746 Leopoldo Retti, a nephew of Frisoni, the Ludwigsburg Court Architect, was commissioned by Duke Carl Eugen to built the New Palace. He built the Baroque garden wing of the palace; then after his death in 1751 work was continued by the Paris architect Louis-Philippe de la Guêpière, who built the wing facing the town and the portico, also in Baroque style. In 1768 R. F. H. Fischer took over the direction of the work; and finally, from 1806 onwards, Nikolaus Thouret completed the palace by building the Neo-classical Planie wing and decorated the interior in Empire style. The New Palace with its 365 rooms thus shows a sequence of styles, from Baroque by way of Rococo and Neo-classicism to Empire.

After the abolition of the monarchy the palace became a museum (1921–39). In 1944 the interior was destroyed by bombing, and although the post-war reconstruction (1956–62) preserved the exterior of the palace in its original form the interior was completely remodelled. It now contains a series of handsome rooms in the central section – the Marble Room, the Round Room, the White Room – which are used by the *Land* Government for State occasions, and also houses part of the Ministry of Education (Planie wing) and Ministry of Finance (garden wing).

Following the model of Versailles, the three wings of the New Palace enclose a grand courtyard. At the entrance to the courtyard are heraldic figures of a stag and a lion (by Anton von Isopi; cast at Wasseralfingen in 1823) on bases by Giovanni Salucci.

Retti's garden wing, overlooking the rose-garden, is still the finest part of the palace, its elegant proportions (with pilasters, projections and an attic storey) giving it particular nobility.

The mezzanine floor of the central range, facing on to the grand

New Palace, garden wing

courtyard, is topped by a balustrade with statues. The double portico with its richly decorated pediment forms an imposing entrance to the palace.

Old Chancellery (Alte Kanzlei)   J12/13(S20)

The Old Chancellery of Dukes Ulrich and Christoph, on the north-east side of Schillerplatz (see entry), was built in 1541–43 and enlarged in 1566. For a long time this handsome four-storey building housed the Rentenkammer (Finance Office), the Land Registry, the Court Pharmacy and various store-rooms for the neighbouring Old Palace (see entry).

The Old Chancellery, with its steeply pitched roof and handsome Renaissance doorways, was badly damaged during the Second World War but after extensive restoration work has now recovered all its old splendour.

In front of it, on the Schlossplatz (see entry) side, is the Mercury Column (1598), originally a water-tower and now crowned by a gilded figure of Mercury (by Ludwig Hofer, 1862).

Location
Schillerplatz 5

U-Bahn
Schlossplatz

Buses
42, 44 (Schlossplatz)

Trams
5, 6, 16 (Schlossplatz)

Old Orphanage (Altes Waisenhaus)   J13(S/T20)

The Old Orphanage (recently renovated) is an irregular Baroque building of four wings surrounding a central courtyard, its façade washed orange-yellow, which was begun in 1705 (architects, P. J. Henisch and J. U. Hein) as a barracks

Location
Charlottenplatz 17

U-Bahn
Charlottenplatz

87

Old Palace

Buses
41–44, 73–77, 7600
(Charlottenplatz)

Trams
1, 2, 4, 5, 6, 15
(Charlottenplatz)

and later completed as an orphanage. The building was extended by R. F. H. Fischer in 1788. It was converted by Paul Schmitthenner in 1922–24 for use as the headquarters of the institute (founded in 1917) which is now the Institute for Relations with other Countries (Institut für Auslandsbeziehungen), a forum for cultural exchange.

Old Palace (Altes Schloss)   J13(S20)

Location
Schillerplatz 6

U-Bahn
Schlossplatz

Buses
42, 44 (Schlossplatz)

Trams
5, 6, 15 (Schlossplatz)

The imposing Old Palace, originally a moated castle built by Count Ulrich I in the 13th c., became the residence of the Counts and Dukes of Württemberg in the 14th c. Between 1553 and 1570, during the time of Dukes Christoph and Ulrich, it was magnificently remodelled in German Renaissance style by Aberlin Tretsch and Blasius and Martin Berwart. In the 18th c. the old moat was filled in. In 1931 part of the palace was destroyed by fire, and in 1944 it suffered heavy damage by bombing. Painstaking restoration work was completed only in 1969. The oldest part of the building is the massive Dürnitz wing, on the south-east side, which was given an additional storey and a terrace in the 16th c.

On the doorway of the Renaissance extension, facing on to Schillerplatz, are the arms (by Simon Schlör, 1570) of Duke Christoph and his wife Anna Maria von Ansbach.

Courtyard

The courtyard, a masterpiece of Renaissance architecture, dates from the extensions to the palace in the mid 16th c. It is surrounded on three sides by three-storey arcades, with fine

Old Palace, south front

Courtyard, Old Palace

fluted columns, depressed arches, balustrades and capitals. At the west end is an equestrian statue of Count Eberhard V (by Ludwig Hofer, 1859).

The courtyard now provides an attractive setting for a variety of cultural events (serenade concerts, etc.).

The round towers at the south-east and south-west corners of the palace were built during the Renaissance extension work; the north-west tower dates from 1687.

Old Palace

20 m
22 yds

1 Doorway
2 Statue of Eberhard V
3 Entrance to
  Württemberg Museum
4 Staircase (for horsemen)
5 Wall-walk
6 Oriel
7 Kunstkammer Tower
8 Archive Room
9 Eberhard Ludwig Tower
10 Clock turret
11 Royal burial vault
12 Sacristy

Old Theatre

Church

The church in the west wing, built by Aberlin Tretsch, was Stuttgart's first Protestant church. The pulpit and altar, in the oriel half-way along the west wall, are given equal prominence. Some pieces of sculpture by Simon Schlör have been preserved. The interior, renovated by Alexander Tritschler in 1865, shows Late Gothic influence.

Under the church is the Royal burial vault (Königsgruft).

See Württemberg Museum.

Old Theatre (Altes Schauspielhaus)

See Königstrasse.

---

*Palace Gardens (Schlossgarten)　　　　F–J13–15(R/S20/21)

The Palace Gardens, which extend from the New Palace to the Neckar bend at Cannstatt, are divided into four parts: the Academy Garden at the south end, the Upper Palace Garden between the New Palace, the Kunstgebäude and the Württemberg State Theatre, the Middle Palace Garden between the Central Station and the Bus Station in the south and Cannstatter Strasse and the old Neckar Gate in the north, and the Lower Palace Garden flanked by Cannstatter Strasse and the Stuttgart–Bad Cannstatt railway.

The creation of this 4 km ($2\frac{1}{2}$ mile) long swathe of open space within the city began in 1805, during the reign of King Friedrich I of Württemberg. It was originally broader than it now is, part of it having been sacrificed over the years to meet the needs of city traffic. On the occasion of the Federal Garden Shows of 1961 and 1977 the gardens were laid out afresh in accordance with the latest ideas on landscape-gardening.

Academy Garden (Akademiegarten)　　　　J13(S20/21)

Trams
1, 2, 4, 5, 6, 15
(Charlottenplatz)

Buses
41–44, 73–77
(Charlottenplatz)

This stretch of gardens occupies the area between Charlottenplatz, the New Palace and the Landtag (see entries). In the centre of the gardens is the Academy Fountain (Akademiebrunnen; by Nikolaus Thouret, 1811), a cast-iron fountain in Empire style, with four lions spouting water, and the Württemberg coat of arms. Near by is a model showing the layout of the old Carlsschule.

Carlsschule

The Academy Garden occupies the site of the old Carlsschule, founded by Duke Carl Eugen in 1770 in the Solitude Palace and moved here in 1775. The school was given the status of a university in 1781. Its best-known pupils were Friedrich Schiller (see Notable Personalities), who trained as an Army doctor here and while at the school wrote his play "Die Räuber" ("The Robbers"), the anatomist Georges Cuvier (1769–1832), the legal scholar Eberhard Wächter (1762–1852), the painter Gottlieb Schick (1776–1812) and the sculpture Johann Heinrich Dannecker (1758–1841).

The school was closed by Duke Ludwig Eugen in 1794, and the building was destroyed during the Second World War.

Lion Fountain

Schiller

Count Eberhard

Horse-Tamer

Palace Gardens

Upper Palace Garden (Oberer Schlossgarten)   H/J13(R/S20/21)

Trams
5, 6, 15 (Schlossplatz)

Buses
42, 44 (Schlossplatz)

The Upper Palace Garden, between the Landtag and Schiller-strasse, was redesigned for the 1961 Federal Garden Show. The central feature is a lake, with a fountain, to the south of which is beautiful rose-garden, with the magnificent garden front of the New Palace (see entry) to the rear. In front of the two houses of the Württemberg State Theatre (see entry) are a number of fine works of sculpture.

Middle Palace Garden (Mittlerer Schlossgarten)   H13(R20/21)

S-Bahn
S 1–6 (Hauptbahnhof/
Arnulf-Klett-Platz)

Buses
40, 42, 43 (Hauptbahnhof/
Arnulf-Klett-Platz)

Trams
5, 6, 9, 14, 15 (Hauptbahnhof/
Arnulf-Klett-Platz)

The Middle Palace Garden, which was also redesigned for the 1961 Federal Garden Show and tidied up for the 1977 Show, is linked with the Upper Garden by an elegant footbridge. At the end of the bridge is a marble group by Paul Müller (1881) depicting Count Eberhard with a shepherd.

Near by, conspicuous with its yellow tent roof, stands the Landespavillon (1977), with exhibitions and displays of information by the *Land* Government (see entry). A few paces away is the ultra-modern Planetarium (see entry).

Lusthaus

Farther north, past a war memorial, we come to the ruins of the Lusthaus (Pleasure House), built by Georg von Beer in Schlossplatz in 1580–93. Reckoned in its day the finest Renaissance building in Germany, it was burned down in 1902 and its remains were re-erected in the Middle Palace Garden in 1904.
Farther north is a lake flanked by a terrace.

Lower Palace Garden (Unterer Schlossgarten)   F–H13–15

Trams
1, 2, 14 (Mineralbäder)

Boat landing-stage
Wilhelma

The Lower Palace Garden was completely redesigned in 1977 and linked with the parks of Villa Berg and Rosenstein Palace (see entries). At the near end of the avenue of plane trees, to the left of the footbridge leading to the Middle Palace Garden, are two marble groups by Hofer, "The Horse-Tamers" (1847). The gardens are attractively laid out with lawns, artificial lakes and a restaurant.

Mineral springs

Two celebrated mineral springs which formerly supplied the Königbad spa establishment, the Hirschquelle (Stag Spring) and the Schwefelquelle (Sulphur Spring), come to the surface here. At the north end of the gardens, where Untere Cannstatter Strasse runs through a tunnel, are the Berger Sprudler (Gushers of Berg – the spa establishment adjoining the gardens) two conical concrete fountains from which water intermittently gushes.

*Planetarium   H13(R21)

Location
Neckarstrasse 47

U-Bahn
Staatsgalerie

The Planetarium conceived by Wilfried Beck-Erlang and built in the Middle Palace Garden in 1977, is one of the most up to date in Europe.
It is a notable example of modern architecture, with its glass-clad roof in the form of a truncated step pyramid suspended on a steel skeleton.

St Martin's Church, Plieningen

In the Dome Room (seating for 300) visitors can watch a "multi-media astro-show" put on with special Zeiss projectors. The foyer of the Planetarium can be used for receptions, and lectures on current developments in astronomy are given in the Kepler Room (seating for 200) and a large seminar room. These rooms are also used by Stuttgart's Communal Cinema.
Presentations: Tues. and Thurs. 10 a.m. and 3 p.m.; Wed. and Fri. 10 a.m., 3 and 8 p.m.; Sat. and Sun. 2, 4 and 6 p.m.

S-Bahn
S 1–6 (Hauptbahnhof)

Buses
40, 42, 43 (Staatsgalerie)

Trams
1, 2, 4, 9, 14 (Staatsgalerie)

Playing-Card Museum

See German Playing-Card Museum.

Plieningen   T14–16

Plieningen, until the 19th c. the largest township in the Filder area to the south of Stuttgart, was incorporated in the city in 1942. It probably takes its name from a noble family which held sway in the Neckar area in the 7th and 8th c. After the Second World War the town, previously a prosperous agricultural community, underwent a major change in social structure, when there was an influx of industrial firms and house-hunters, resulting in a considerable increase in the area of the town.

Buses
70, 73, 74, 75, 76

Trams
3 (Garbe)

St Martin's Church (Protestant) was built in Romanesque style in the 12th c., during the reign of Duke Welf VI. There are

St Martin's Church

Already a legend: the Porsche 356 of 1948

interesting relief carvings under the eaves. The Gothic choir was built in 1493.

The west tower, with a steeple, is 14th c., but was added to in 1765.

Mönchshof and Town Hall

The Old Town Hall (Altes Rathaus), which together with St Martin's Church, the presbytery and the old Mönchshof forms an interesting and picturesque grouping, is a handsome half-timbered building erected in 1748–51. It now houses a local museum (Plieninger Heimatmuseum; open Sat. and Sun. 10 a.m.–noon), with material ranging from prehistoric and early historical times to the present day.

*Porsche Museum

Location
Porsche-Werk II,
Porschestrasse 42,
Stuttgart-Zuffenhausen

S-Bahn
S 4–6 (Zuffenhausen)

Buses
52, 90, 99 (Porsche)

The Porsche Museum, opened in 1976, gives a comprehensive survey of the history of the world-famed racing and sports-car firm, founded by Ferdinand Porsche in Zuffenhausen in 1931. Full explanations and illustrative material are displayed. The exhibits include production sports models and racing cars, including an 1100 h.p. CanAm, which will fascinate motor-racing enthusiasts; a 1922 Austro-Daimler Sascha for the nostalgic; production and racing engines and gearboxes; and even an early aircraft engine of 1913.

Opening times: Mon.–Fri. 9 a.m.–noon and 1.30–4 p.m.

Postal History Collection H12(R20)
(Postgeschichtliche Sammlung)

This exhibition, mounted by the Telecommunications Department of the Post Office, illustrates very effectively the development of telecommunications. Some of the exhibits in the collection, which has been built up since 1908, have been used in the past for the training of telecommunications staff and are still in full working order.

The prize exhibit is the first telephone, invented by Graham Bell. Beside it can be seen the first wall telephones designed by the Royal Württemberg Telegraph Workshops and the first Stuttgart radio transmitter, which began to operate in 1924. Another interesting item is the first Stuttgart telephone exchange.

The extensive collections of material on the history of the postal services are at present in store and not accessible to the public.

Location
Friedrichstrasse 13

U-Bahn
Hauptbahnhof (Arnulf-Klett-Platz)

S-Bahn
S 1–6 (Hauptbahnhof)

Buses
A, 40, 42, 43
(Hauptbahnhof/Arnulf-Klett-Platz)

Opening times
Temporarily closed

Pragfriedhof (Cemetery) F/G13

The Pragfriedhof, Stuttgart's first municipal cemetry, was opened in 1872. Among the notable people buried here are the writers Karl Gerok, Cäsar Flaischlen and Eduard Mörike, the airship-constructor Count Zeppelin, the Nobel Prize-winner Hans Spemann and the celebrated cabaret artiste Claire Waldoff (1884–1957).

The chapel in the Neo-Gothic entrance block on Friedhofstrasse was designed by the Ulm architect A. Beyer (1873–76). The crematorium (by W. Scholter, 1907, with an extension of 1983) is an unusual variant of Jugendstil (Art Nouveau) architecture.

Location
Friedhofstrasse 44

Tram
5 (Pragfriedhof)

Prinzenbau (Prince's Palace) J12(S20)

The Prinzenbau was begun in 1605 by the great architect of the period, Heinrich Schickhardt, but was completed only in 1715 (by Johann Friedrich Nette). The façade shows Italian (Palladian) influence. After many changes of use – it was occupied for a time by Wilhelmine von Graevenitz, Duke Eberhard Ludwig's influential mistress – the palace became the residence of the Princes of Württemberg. The future King Wilhelm II, Württemberg's last monarch, was born here in 1848. The palace, which was badly damaged during the Second World War, now houses part of the Ministry of Justice of Baden-Württemberg.

Location
Schillerplatz 4

U-Bahn
Schlossplatz

S-Bahn
S 1–6 (Stadtmitte)

Buses
42, 44 (Schlossplatz)

Trams
5, 6, 15 (Schlossplatz)

Rack railway (Zahnradbahn) L–N12

Stuttgart's rack railway began to operate in 1884, when the cars were pushed uphill by a steam-engine. The railway, 2 km (1¼ miles) long, runs from Marienplatz in the southern part of the city to Degerloch (see entry), 205 m (673 ft) higher. The steepest gradient on the line, which runs up alongside the Alte

Route
Marienplatz-Degerloch

Tram
10 (Marienplatz)

Rack Railway

Weinsteige, is 17.3 per cent. In the old station at Degerloch are a number of veteran rail-cars.

*Roman Lapidarium (Römisches Lapidarium)   J13(S20)

Location
Old Palace, Schillerplatz

U-Bahn
Schlossplatz

The Roman Lapidarium, a branch of the Württemberg Museum (see entry), is housed in the Old Palace in Schillerplatz (see entries). It contains stone monuments and fragments found in Württemberg, mainly milestones, columns, reliefs and altars. Among the most notable exhibits are the following: an altar of

Rosenstein Palace, north-east front

Vulcan from Benningen (Ludwigsburg district); an altar of Jupiter from Metzingen (Reutlingen district); an altar of the Four Goddesses of the Way from Cannstatt; milestones from the Roman road from Grinario (now Köngen, in Esslingen district) to Sumelocenna (Rottenburg, Tübingen district) 129 B.C.; the gravestone of Ingenuus (with relief of a funeral banquet), from Cannstatt; a Jupiter and Giant group from Hausen an der Zaber, A.D. 200.

A diorama with tin figures gives a vivid impression of the Roman settlement in the Cannstatt area.

These are periodic special exhibitions and displays of new material recovered by the State Archaeological Department.

Buses
42, 44 (Schlossplatz)

Trams
5, 6, 15 (Schlossplatz)

Opening times
Tues. and Thurs.–Sun.
10 a.m.–5 p.m., Wed.
10 a.m.–7 p.m.

Rosenstein Palace (Schloss Rosenstein)   F15

This imposing palace, situated on the high ground to the west of the Neckar bend at Cannstatt, was built for King Wilhelm I by the Court Architect, Giovanni Salucci, and completed in 1829. Burned out in 1944 and rebuilt in 1950, it now houses the State Museum of Natural History (see entry). Between the wars it was occupied by the World War Library.

The palace is a long single-storey building in Late Neo-classical style with porticoes in the manner of Greek temples; the sculpture in the pediments depicts heroic mythological scenes. In front of the central portico are figures of lions (by Güldenstein and Pelargus, 1852).

The palace, conceived as a "royal country house", has a total of seventy-four rooms. In the banqueting hall is a frieze by Konrad Weitbrecht (1796–1836), restored, depicting the rustic year and seasons.

The palace park with an area of some 100 hectares (250 acres), is one of the most beautiful in Stuttgart. It was laid out in the 19th c. in the style of an English landscaped park and originally planted with native and exotic deciduous trees. Coniferous trees, including wellingtonias from California, began to be planted in 1838.

Particularly attractive is the rose-garden, with its charming pieces of sculpture, on the east side of the palace, which impressed even Bismarck.

The east end of the park is occupied by the Wilhelma Gardens (see entry). At the north-west corner of the park is the new building of the State Museum of Natural History (see entry).

The park contains a notable work by the Feuerbach sculptress Susanne Knorr, "Squatting Woman". In front of the palace are figures by Doris Schmauder (1982) modelled on Dannecker's nymphs.

Location
Rosenstein 14

S-Bahn
S 1–3 (Bad Cannstatt)

Trams
1, 2, 14 (Mineralbäder),
14 (Wilhelma)

Boat landing-stage
Wilhelma

Opening times
Tues.–Fri. 10 a.m.–4 p.m.,
Sat. and Sun. 10 a.m.–5 p.m.

Rosenstein Park

Rotebühlplatz   J12(T18/19)

Rotebühlplatz, a busy traffic intersection, takes its name from a red sacred image (*rotes bild*) to be seen in the square as late as the 15th c. In the 17th c. a mail transfer office (part of the postal service run by the Princes of Thurn und Taxis) was established here.

At the corner of Calwer Strasse (see entry) stands the old

S-Bahn
S 1–6 (Stadtmitte)

U-Bahn
Rotebühlplatz

St Eberhard's Church

Hans-im-Gluck-Brunnen

palace of the Freiherren (Barons) von Gültingen (18th c.; now the Paulaner Restaurant). In front of it is a fountain (the Postplatzbrunnen) by Nikolaus Thouret (1820).

On the west side of the square rises the Rotebühlbau, built in 1827–43 as a barracks, with two side wings projecting at right angles from the main block. It is now occupied by the Stuttgart Finance Department and the Minstry of Labour and Social Affairs.

St Barbara's Church, Hofen

Location
Wolfgangstrasse 6,
Stuttgart-Hofen

Bus
54 (Hofen)

Tram
14 (Hofen)

St Barbara's Church, built in 1783–84, during the reign of Duke Carl Eugen, is one of Stuttgart's few Baroque buildings. Its stucco-work shows Rococo influences. It has a very beautiful carved image of the Virgin (*c.* 1500), which until quite recent times drew large numbers of pilgrims.

Until the transfer of St Eberhard's Church from Solitude to the lower part of Königstrasse (see entries), St Barbara's was much used by Stuttgart's Catholics for christenings and marriages.

St Eberhard's Church (Eberhardskirche)   J13(S20)

Location
Königstrasse 7

U-Bahn
Schlossplatz

St Eberhard's, Stuttgart's first Roman Catholic parish church, was transferred from Solitude (see entry) to its present site in 1808–11 on the order of King Friedrich I. Originally Baroque, it was remodelled in Neo-classical style by Nikolaus Thouret.

The church was destroyed by bombing in 1944, and was rebuilt in its present form in 1953–55 by Hugo Schlösser. The red sandstone exterior has gained from the insertion of a circular window with a cross, depicting Christ and the Twelve Apostles. The tower is a two-stage open-work metal structure. The interior is plain. Over the altar is a large gold relief of Christ, and a beautiful gilded Pietà. The Albiez organ, the largest in Stuttgart, was consecrated in 1982.

In 1978 St Eberhard's Co-Cathedral of the Rottenburg-Stuttgart diocese.

S-Bahn
S 1–6 (Hauptbahnhof)

Buses
42, 44 (Schlossplatz)

Trams
5, 6, 15 (Schlossplatz)

St John's Church (Johanneskirche am Feuersee)   K11

The Neo-Gothic Church of St John, designed by Christian von Leins (1865–76), stands on a peninsula in the Feuersee (Fire Lake), an artificial lake which acts as a water-storage tank for fire-fighting. In both plan and elevation and in the pattern of architectural forms Leins very successfully reflected the High Gothic of France. After suffering heavy damage during the Second World War the church was rebuilt in 1948, without its spire.

Location
Gutenbergstrasse 11

S-Bahn
S 1–6 (Feuersee)

Buses
41, 44, 92 (Feuersee)

---

*St Leonard's Church (Leonhardskirche)   K13(T20)

This Late Gothic church was begun in 1463 under the direction of Aberlin Jörg. The choir is older, indicating that there was an earlier sacred building on the site, perhaps a chapel dedicated to St Leonard.

After suffering heavy damage during the Second World War the church was rebuilt in 1948–54 by R. Lempp, with new windows by Kohler.

The choir-stalls (c. 1500) are from the old Dominican church, now the Hospital Church (see entry). There is also a fine modern Crucifix (by K. Hemeter, 1957). The humanist Johannes Reuchlin is buried in the church.

St Leonard's was again renovated in 1982–83. The front of the gallery has paintings by Yelin.

Location
Leonhardsplatz 26

U-Bahn
Rathaus

Buses
41, 44, 84, 85, 87, 92, 93, 7945 (Rathaus)

Trams
1, 2, 4 (Rathaus)

St Mary's Church (Marienkirche)   K12

This Roman Catholic church was built between 1871 and 1879 to the design of J. Egle, who took St Elizabeth's Church in Marburg as his model. The two 60 m (200 ft) high towers give this Neo-Gothic church a powerful and imposing effect.

Location
Tübinger Strasse 36

U-Bahn
Osterreichischer Platz

St Nicholas's Church (St Nikolaus)   H11

St Nicholas's is one of Stuttgart's two major Russian Orthodox places of worship, the other being the burial chapel on the Rotenberg (see Württemberg). The foundation-stone of the church, the initiative for which came from the Grand Princess and Duchess Vera Konstantinovna, widow of Duke Eugen of

Location
Kornbergstrasse 20 B

Bus
40 (Russische Kirche)

St Vitus's Chapel   Mühlhausen

(1380–85)

South wall   Choir arch   North wall

GROUND-PLAN

A Tower B Nave C Choir
1 Entrance (outside, inscription recording start of building)
2 High Altar (1510). (The original Mühlhausen Altar, painted in Prague in 1385, is in the State Gallery). In shrine (left to right): SS. Modestus (Vitus's teacher), Sigismund, Vitus (with cauldron), Wenceslas, Hippolytus.
3 Font
4 Pulpit (1957)
5 North altar (no side panels; under stone canopy); from left to right SS. Catherine, Dorothy, Barbara, Walpurga and Agatha
6 South altar (with painted side panels; under stone canopy); in shrine John the Baptist, flanked by Paul (left) and Peter (right)
7 Monument of Jakon von Kaltental (d. 1555; figure by Jakob Woller)
8 Monument of the last Kaltental of the Mühlhausen line (d. 1586; epitaph by Sem Schlör)
9 Monument of Engelbold von Kaltental (d. 1558; possibly by a local stonemason)
10 Gravestones (badly worn)
11 Organ (1950; in gallery)

WALL PAINTINGS IN CHOIR

I Legend of St Vitus
  I1 Vitus is beaten by his father Hylas
  I2 Vitus in front of the Emperor Valerian
  I3 Vitus cures his torturers
  I4 Vitus is made to dance (girls)
  I5 Girls (=angels) blind Hylas
  I6 Vitus flees overseas with his teachers
  I7 Vitus cures a prince in Rome
  I8 Vitus boiled in pitch or oil
  I9 Vitus leaves the cauldron unscathed
  I10 Vitus is thrown to a lion, which does not harm him
  I11 Vitus is hanged with his teachers
  I12 The nun Florentia buries the dead

II Life of the Virgin
  II1 Annunciation
  II2 Marriage of Mary and Joseph
  II3 Visitation
  II4 Adoration of Magi
  II5 Death of the Virgin

III Madonna with the Sheltering Cloak
  The Virgin spreads her cloak over the people who seek refuge under it

IV Other paintings at east end of choir
  IV1a St Sigismund
  IV1b St Sigismund and his family are drowned
  IV2a St Wenceslas
  IV2b St Wenceslas is murdered at the instigation of his brother
  IV3/4 St Michael

V Last Judgment
  V1 Christ (on a double rainbow) judges the world; on either side the Virgin and John the Baptist
  V2 Peter at the gate of Paradise
  In the adjoining vaulting, angels with trumpets and instruments of torture; at end of choir Evangelists and Fathers of the Church

Tram
4 (Russische Kirche)

Württemberg, was laid on 18 May 1895, the twenty-seventh birthday of Tsar Nicholas II, and the church was consecrated on 6 December (St Nicholas's Day) in the same year. The church was destroyed during the Second World War but was rebuilt in 1950.

*St Vitus's Chapel (Veitskapelle)

Location
Meierberg 16,
Stuttgart-Mühlhausen

Bus
54 (Mühlhausen)

The Gothic Chapel of St Vitus in Mühlhausen was built in the 1380s by Reinhard von Mühlhausen, a burgher of Prague. This little village church is one of the most beautiful in Stuttgart, with a striking rectangular tower and a choir closed on three sides. Note the very fine tracery in both parts of

St Vitus's Chapel, Mülhausen

the church. The church became Protestant in the second half of the 16th c.

Tram
14 (Mühlhausen)

The finely carved Late Gothic altar-piece, with side panels, replaced (1510) an earlier and simpler altar-piece painted in Prague in 1385, now in the State Gallery (see entry). The predella, with Christ and the Apostles, is particulary fine. In the shrine, under gilded foliage decoration, are figures of St Modestus (St Vitus's teacher), St Sigismund with his crown, sword and imperial orb, and St Hippolytus. Above can be seen the three martyr saints, Vitus in his cauldron, Stephen and Lawrence. The side panels depict scenes from St Vitus's life.

High Altar

The wall-paintings, skilfully restored in 1974, are of remarkable quality. The twelve paintings of 1428 between the capitals and the cornice relate the legend of St Vitus. Above the windows are five scenes from the life of the Virgin. On the north wall is a wonderful Virgin holding out her sheltering cloak (Schutzmantelmadonna). Other paintings at the east end of the choir depict SS. Sigismund, Wenceslas and Michael. Over the choir arch is a Last Judgment.
There are also some fine frescoes in the crypt.

Wall-paintings

The right-hand side altar, beautifully carved, has figures of John the Baptist, Peter and Paul. Hanging on the wall are finely painted side panels.
The left-hand side altar, also carved, has figures of the female martyrs Barbara, Dorothy, Walpurga, Catherine and Agatha.
The monuments of the Kaltental family date from the 16th c.
The oil-painting of Frau Magdalena von Closen is from St Walpurga's Church, destroyed during the Second World War (tower, 1390).

Side altars

Schellenturm

The Schellenturm . . .   *. . . and its hospitable interior*

*Schellenturm   K13(T20)

Location
Weberstrasse 72

U-Bahn
Rathaus

Buses
41–44, 84, 85, 87, 92, 93
(Rathaus)

Trams
1, 2, 4 (Rathaus)

The Schellenturm, built in 1564, is the last relic of the old town walls. The name comes from the *Schellen* (fetters) worn by criminals confined in the tower. The tower was destroyed in 1944, but the lower part was restored in 1963 and the half-timbered upper floor with its pointed roof rebuilt in 1979–80, thanks to the efforts of local people concerned to maintain the heritage of the past.

The tower is now occupied by a romantic wine-bar much frequented both by Stuttgarters and visitors.

**Schillerplatz   J12/13(S20)

U-Bahn
Schlossplatz

Buses
42, 44 (Schlossplatz)

Trams
5, 6, 15 (Schlossplatz)

Since the completion in 1977 of an extensive programme of building and renovation the Schillerplatz has been the very heart of Stuttgart, presenting a particularly lively scene on market days.

On the south-east side of the square is the massive bulk of the Old Palace, housing the Württemberg Museum (see entries).

On the south-west side stands the Stiftskirche, and adjoining this the Fruchtkasten (see entries), behind which can be seen the elegant ultra-modern glass staircase tower of the Commerzbank extension (by H. Kammerer and W. Belz, 1972).

On the north-west side of the square is the Prinzenbau (see entry) and to the north-east of this the Old Chancellery (see entry), with the Mercury Column (1598) in front of it.

Market day in Schillerplatz

Commerzbank, staircase tower

In the centre of the square is a monument to Schiller by the Danish sculptor Berthel Thorvaldsen; it stands on a base designed by Nikolaus Thouret. The monument was unveiled on 8 May 1859 in the presence of Thouret and Schiller's grandson.

Schiller Monument

*Schlossplatz

The spacious Schlossplatz, lying between the area round the Central Station and the old core of the city, was completely redesigned for the 1977 Federal Garden Show by the architectural firm of Behnisch & Partners. It is bounded on the south-east by the New Palace, on the south-west by the Old Palace and on the north-west by the Königsbau and the Kleiner Schlossplatz (see entries). On its north side are the Olgabau and the Kunstgebäude (see entry).

U-Bahn
Schlossplatz

Buses
42, 44 (Schlossplatz)

Trams
5, 6, 15 (Schlossplatz)

In front of the Königsbau, over the new U-Bahn station, is a handsome and richly decorated cast-iron bandstand of 1871 which originally stood in front of the New Palace.

The central feature of the square is the Jubilee Column (by J. M. Knapp), erected in 1841 to mark King Wilhelm I's silver jubilee (twenty-five years on the throne) and crowned in 1863 with a 5 m (16½ ft) high bronze allegory of Concordia by Hofer. The finely carved reliefs on the base (by T. von Wagner) depict the homage of the Estates and Crown Prince Wilhelm as a participant in the Wars of Liberation of 1814.

Jubilee Column

The Schlossplatz and the New Palace

On either side of the Jubilee Column are fountains designed by Christian Leins, with figures by Kopp.

Statue of Duke Christoph

At the north-west corner of the square is a bronze statue (by Paul Müller, 1889) of Duke Christoph, commissioned by King Karl on his silver jubilee to commemorate the ruler who established the pattern of Church organisation and education in Württemberg.

Schwabenzentrum (Swabian Centre)   K12/13(T19/20)

Location
Hauptstätter Strasse 40

U-Bahn
Rathaus

Buses
41–44, 84, 85, 87, 92, 93
(Rathaus)

Trams
1, 2, 4 (Rathaus)

The first section of this office and commercial complex (designed by Kilpper & Partners) was opened in 1980. Within the last few years a large clearance programme has been under way to remove numbers of unsightly and sub-standard buildings put up after the last war and to replace them by this ultra-modern complex. The finely articulated façades are extremely effective with their cladding of glass, bronze sheeting and travertine. In the entrance lobby of the south block is a sculpture, "Leaning Woman", by the Feuerbach sculptress Susanne Knorr. In the courtyard can be seen a metal structure resembling a prawn's tail.

Silberburg Gardens (Silberburganlage)   K11/12

Bus: 41 (Marienstrasse/
Silberburgstrasse)

The Silberburg Gardens, now dominated by the offices of the Allianz insurance corporation, were originally the park of an

18th c. country house which later became a much-frequented inn. The gardens were beautifully laid out for the 1961 Federal Garden Show, with attractive flower-beds, playing areas and fountains.

From the Silberburg Gardens a corridor of green extends up to the Karlshöhe (342 m (1,122 ft)), from which there are superb panoramic views of the Stuttgart Basin. The hill is named after King Karl, who had the flat hilltop laid out as a garden in 1889. On the north-west slope of the hill, at the lower end of the Hasenbergsteige, is the Gänsepeterbrunnen (Peter the Goose-Boy Fountain; by Bausch, 1901).

Karlshöhe

*Solitude   H5

This little country palace to the west of the city centre, standing on a hill (497 m (1,631 ft)) in the Glemswald was built for Duke Carl Eugen as a "maison de plaisance" between 1763 and 1767. The architects were Philippe de la Guêpière and Johann Friedrich Weyhing, following plans drawn up by the Duke himself.
The palace comprises a ballroom, flanking pavilions, stabling, servants' quarters and a chapel. A dead straight road, taken as the base-line for the Württemberg ordnance survey, runs from Solitude to Ludwigsburg Palace, 15 km (9 miles) north-east. Only a few years after its completion Solitude was allowed to fall into a state of neglect and dilapidation, and much

Location
Solitude 1

Bus
92 (Solitude)

Opening times
Tues.–Sun. 9 a.m.–12 noon and 1.30–5 p.m.

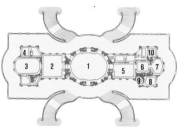

Solitude

1	White Room	6	Marble Room
2	Assembly Room	7	Palm Room
3	Music Room	8	Writing Cabinet
4	Red Cabinet	9	Library
5	Ante-room	10	Bedroom

renovation work has had to be carried out over the subsequent two centuries.

The palace creates an effect of monumentality, mainly because of the massive colonnaded substructure. Equally impressive is the domed central oval, flanked by single-storey wings. Dignity is added by the pilasters which articulate the façade and the window ornaments. The effect is enhanced by the colouring, recently restored to the original pale yellow wash.

Interior

The interior is in a style transitional between Rococo and Neo-classicism – a style reflected both in the architecture and the decoration. Duke Carl Eugen acquired the furnishings (furniture, pictures, porcelain) about 1770. The ceiling-paintings by N. Guibal and the recently discovered frescoes in the basement are masterpieces of their kind.

Chapel

The Early Neo-classical chapel, at the end of the eastern arm of the curving range of subsidiary buildings, has double columns supporting the roof and is decorated with fine stucco-work and a magnificent ceiling-painting of the Ascension by Guibal. The painting of Moses with the Tables of the Law in the sacristy is also by Guibal.

Cemetery

In the cemetery of the palace are the graves of the sculptor Fritz von Graevenitz and the choreographer John Cranko.

The Carlsschule, originally founded in 1770 as a military orphanage, was moved to the Schlossgarten (see entry) in Stuttgart in 1775.

Solitude car-racing circuit: See Glemswald.

South German Radio (Süddeutscher Rundfunk, SDR) G15

Location
Neckarstrasse 230

Trams
1, 2, 14 (Stöckach)

Pferdle and Äffle

The South German Radio Corporation, the first transmitter of which began operating in 1924, moved into its present headquarters, a complex of three tower blocks designed by R. Gutbrod, in 1976.

Block A (seventeen storeys) houses the Director's office and administrative departments. In Block B are various technical departments and the music division. Block C contains the programme directorate and the individual programme sections (politics, economic affairs, culture, music) with their sub-divisions (e.g. current affairs, rural interests, schools broadcasts, etc.). A short distance away, in the Villa Berg (see entry), are the studios.

Two very popular figures are the cartoon characters Pferdle and Äffle (Horsy and Monk) who feature in South German Radio's television advertisements. Their spiritual father is the graphic artist Armin Lang, who also writes and speaks their dialogues, in the broadest of Swabian dialect.

Spitalkirche

See Hospital Church

Stäffele (lanes, footpaths)

The slopes of the hills round the Stuttgart Basin are covered
with a network of well over 400 steep footpaths and stepped
lanes, with a total length of almost 30 km (19 miles), known to
native Stuttgarters as *stäffele*. Many of them date from a time
when the hillsides were terraced and cultivated as vineyards
and gardens. In later times, when the terraces were built-up as
Stuttgart expanded, the lanes provided useful short-cuts to the
city centre. During the winter the local children use them as
slides. One of the longest and steepest of these lanes, on the
Hasenberg, climbs some 240 m (790 ft), with 308 steps: hence,
perhaps, the name of "Hasenberg-Tiroler" by which the people
of Stuttgart are widely known.

Stammheim

Stammheim (pop. 10,000), Stuttgart's most northerly ward,
which was incorporated in the city in 1942, lies on the southern
edge of the fertile Langes Feld area. It is traversed by the
Solitude–Allee, the road which runs in a straight line from
Ludwigsburg to Solitude and formed a base-line for the land
surveyors of Württemberg.

Bus
7768 (Stammheim Rathaus)

Tram
5 (Stammheim)

The old Schloss (palace) of Stammheim was built in 1580 to
the design of Heinrich Schickhardt, replacing an older moated
castle which had been the seat of the local ruling family, who
came from Berg (Cannstatt). This imposing building is now an
old people's home.

Schloss

The church has a medieval choir with reticulated vaulting
(1488). Heraldic gravestones of the Stammheim family.

Church

In the Emerholz sports complex, on the north-western outskirts
of Stammheim, the largest tennis centre in Europe is under
construction – reflecting the popularity of this form of sport in
the Middle Neckar region.

Emerholz sports complex

Stammheim's fortress-like prison, built in the 1970s, has a
court-room included in the complex, and Stammheim hit the
world's headlines when the Baader-Meinhof trials were held
here. In October 1977 three members of the gang (Andreas
Baader, Jan-Carl Raspe and Gudrun Ensslin) were found dead
in their cells.

Prison

State Academy of Art (Staatliche Akademie der bildenden Künste)   F12

The State Academy of Art, successor to the Académie des Arts
founded by Duke Carl Eugen in 1761, has been housed since
1912 in a building at Weissenhof designed by Eisenlohr and
Pankok, with a 1960s extension by Aichele, Policard &
Partners.
The Academy has established a solid reputation. Artists who
have taught here include Landenberger, Hoelzel and
Baumeister.

Location
Am Weissenhof 1

Bus
43 (Kunstakademie)

State Archives (Hauptstaatsarchiv) J13(S21)

Location
Konrad-Adenauer-Strasse 4

U-Bahn
Charlottenplatz

Buses
41–44, 73, 77, 7600
(Charlottenplatz)

Trams
1, 2, 4, 5, 6 (Charlottenplatz)

Opening times
Reading room: Mon.–Thurs.
9 a.m.–5.15 p.m., Fri. 9 a.m.
–3.45 p.m.
Issue of archive material:
Mon.–Fri. 9–11 a.m. and
1–3.30 p.m.

The State Archives, one of the largest archive collections in the Federal Republic, occupies a cube-shaped modern building completed in 1969. It contains documents on the history of Württemberg covering a period of more than a thousand years. Here, available for consultation, are the archives of the Duchy of Württemberg, the ministries and central departments of the kingdom of Württemberg and its successor the province (*Land*) of Württemberg, and the ministerial archives of the present federal *Land* of Baden-Württemberg.

Among the treasures to be seen here is the original of the Papal Bull (issued by Pope Leo X on 15 June 1520) threatening Martin Luther with excommunication.

Special exhibitions on particular themes are put on here from time to time, and attract large numbers of visitors.

State Gallery (Staatsgalerie) J13(R/S21)

Location
Konrad-Adenauer-Strasse
30–32

The State Gallery is one of the finest art collections in the Federal Republic. The section devoted to 20th c. paintings enjoys an international reputation. The original building, or Old Gallery, was designed by Gottlob Georg Barth in Neo-classical

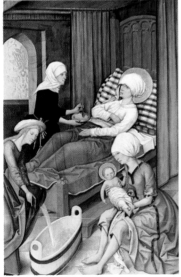

Pfullendorf Altar (detail)

Oskar Schlemmer, "Triadic Ballet"

State Gallery

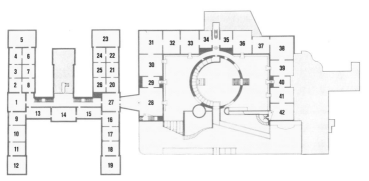

UPPER FLOOR

1, 9–12 Early German painting
2–8 Italian painting

13–15 Dutch and Flemish painting
16–27 19th c.

28–35 Modern schools
36–42 Contemporary art

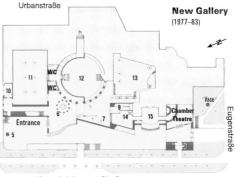

Old Gallery
(1838–42; enlarged
1881–88; rebuilt
1958)

Urbanstraße

New Gallery
(1977–83)

Wagenburgtunnel

King Wilhelm I

Entrance

Eugenstraße

Konrad-Adenauer-Straße

GROUND FLOOR

1 20th c. art in south-west Germany
2 Graphic Collection, changing exhibitions
3 Café
4 Cloakroom and sales counter
5 Henry Moore, "Draped Reclining Woman" (1957–58)

6 Sales counter
7 Cloakroom
8 Stairs up
9 Stairs up
10 Hugo Borst Room
11 Changing exhibitions

12 Sculpture Court
13 Film and lecture theatre
14 Glass lift
15 Fresko café-restaurant

State Gallery

Extension to State Gallery (part view)

U-Bahn
Staatsgalerie

S-Bahn
S 1–6 (Hauptbahnhof)

Buses
40, 42, 43 (Staatsgalerie)

Trams
1, 2, 4, 9, 14 (Staatsgalerie)

Opening times
Tues.–Sun. 10 a.m.–5 p.m.,
Tues. and Thurs. until 8 p.m.

style and built in 1838–42; originally consisting of three wings set round a forecourt, it was enlarged in 1881–88 by the addition of two wings at the back. In the forecourt is an equestrian statue of King Wilhelm I.

Adjoining the Old Gallery to the south is James Stirling's New Gallery, faced with travertine (1977–83), a masterpiece of contemporary architecture. The central feature of the new building is a rotunda, which is enclosed by three wings with roofs designed to admit the maximum of light.

Only a selection of outstanding works from this rich collection can be mentioned:

Early German paintings, 14th–16th c.

Prague Altar, from St Vitus's Chapel, Mühlhausen; Pfullendorf Altar; Zeitblom, "St Florian"; Ratgeb, Herrenberg Altar; Holbein the Elder, "Madonna with Donor"; Cranach the Elder, "Judith".

Italian painting, 14th–18th c.

Erbach Panels ("Apocalypse", by an unknown Neapolitan master); Canaletto, "View of the Brenta from Dolo"; Carpaccio, "Stoning of St Stephen".

Dutch and Flemish painting, 15th–17th c.

Memling, "Bathsheba in her Bath"; Hals, "half-Length Portrait of a Man"; Rembrandt, "Paul in Prison"; Rubens, "Old Lady with Child"; Ruisdael, "Egmond aan Zee".

Swabian Neo-classicists

Hetsch, "Mother of the Gracchi"; Schick, "Frau von Cotta".

European painting 19th c.

Burne-Jones, "Perseus Cycle"; Cézanne, "Bathers in Front of

Tent"; Corinth, "Self-Portrait"; Corot, "Girl with Red Flower"; Courbet, "Madame Maquet"; Delacroix, "Indian Woman attacked by a Tiger"; Feuerbach, "Iphigenia"; Friedrich, "Bohemian Landscape"; Gauguin, "Where are you going?"; Liebermann, "Old Men's Home"; Monet, "Fields in Spring"; Renoir, "Madame Choquet".

Baselitz, "Eagle"; Baumeister, "Primeval Figures", "Gilgamesh Cycle"; Beckman, "Self-Portrait with Red Shawl", "Peruvian Soldier drinking"; Braque, "Violin"; de Chirico, "Metaphysical Interior with Factory"; Dalí, "The Sublime Moment"; Dix, "Match-Seller"; Dubuffet, "Porte Paysanne"; Duchamp, "Study for a Chocolate-Mill"; Ernst, "Sainte Cécilie"; Grosz, "Funeral"; Hodler, "Return from Marignano"; Kandinsky, "Improvisation 9"; Kiefer, "The World Ash"; Kirchner, "Berlin Street"; Klee, "Red Houses on Hill", "Music Underground"; Klein, "Monochrome Bleu"; Kokoschka, "Woman in Blue"; Léger, "Playing Cards"; Matisse, "Woman at her Toilet"; Mondrian, "Composition in Red and Blue"; Munch, "Four girls"; Nolde, "Dancers"; Picasso, "Artistes", "Violin", "Seated Woman"; Schlemmer, "Plan with Figures", "Railings"; Wols, "Composition".

European painting, 20th c.

Newman, "Who's afraid of Red, Yellow and Blue?"; Pollock, "Out of the Web"; Rauschenberg, "Spot"; Reinhardt, "Abstract Painting"; Warhol, "Peach Halves".

American painting since 1945

Andre, "Steel Bar"; Arp, "Star Navel"; Beuys, "dernier espace"; Calder, "Mobile"; Giacometti, "Standing Woman"; Hanson, "Charwoman"; Kienholz, "The Birthday"; Kricke, "Large F VI"; Lehmbruck, "Climbing Youth"; Lipchitz, "Head"; Maillol, "Head of Venus"; Merz, "Double Igloo"; Moore, "Helmeted Head 2"; Schlemmer, "Triadic Ballet"; Segal, "Girl sitting against a Wall"; Serra, "Dead"; Tinguely, "The Electro-Ironic Brain"; Picasso, "Bathers"; Rodin, "Iris"; Rückriem, "Dolomite".

20th c. sculpture

Some 300,000 items: drawings of all periods, printed graphics. The collection is particularly strong in the following fields: the Baroque period in Bologna and Genoa; Giambattista and Domenico Tiepolo; Max Kade Collection of older printed graphics; international graphic art of the 20th c.; French illustrated books; Jugendstil (Art Nouveau) posters.

Graphic Collection

State Mint (Staatliche Münze) F17

The State Mint occupies a modern building in Bad Cannstatt adjoining the Criminal Investigation Department (Landeskriminalamt). A considerable proportion of the coins circulating in the Federal Republic are minted here. (The mint from which a coin comes can be identified by the letter stamped on one side: F for Stuttgart, D for Munich, G for Karlsruhe, J for Hamburg.) The Stuttgart Mint also produces coins for some Asian and Latin American countries.

Württemberg acquired the right to mint its own coins in the 14th c., by virtue of a privilege granted to Count Eberhard II by the Emperor Charles IV.

Location
Taubenheimstrasse 77,
Stuttgart-Bad Cannstatt

S-Bahn
S 1–3 (Bad Cannstatt)

Trams
1, 13 (Augsburger Platz)

*State Museum of Natural History   F15
(Staatliches Museum für Naturkunde)

Location
Schloss Rosenstein,
Rosenstein 14,
Stuttgart-Bad Cannstatt

Trams
14 (Wilhelma),
1, 2, 14 (Mineralbäder)

Boat landing-stage
Wilhelma

The State Museum of Natural History, housed in Rosenstein Palace (see entry) and a recently completed new building, is one of the leading museums of its kind in Central Europe, with valuable collections in the fields of mineralogy, geology, botany and zoology.

The origins of the museum go back to a natural history collection in the Duke of Württemberg's Kunstkammer (Art Gallery) in the 16th c., which Duke Carl Eugen developed into a separate Cabinet of Natural History in 1791. In 1822 the collection was housed in a building of its own at the corner of Neckarstrasse and Archivstrasse. After suffering much destruction during the Second World War it was dispersed to some

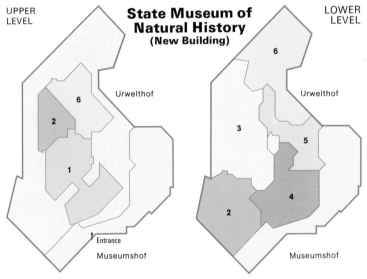

DEPARTMENTS IN NEW BUILDING

1 Prologue:
Introduction to the history of the earth and of life

2 Triassic:
Dinosaurs from the Muschelkalk and Keuper of South-west Germany

3 Liassic:
The Holzmaden site; fossils from the Poseidonian schists of the Liassic

4 Jurassic:
The Middle and Upper Jurassic in Württemberg; ammonites and invertebrates

5 Tertiary:
The Tertiary in Württemberg; small vertebrates, invertebrates; plant impressions; dinotherium skeletons

6 Quaternary:
Ice Age site; Ice Age finds in Baden-Württemberg

Selected collections of material are displayed in Rosenstein Palace, at the south-east corner of the park.

Stork's nest

twenty or thirty different places in Germany, until in 1950 part of the collection was accommodated in Rosenstein Palace.

The museum offers a survey of the evolution of animal species, displays the fauna of south-western Germany (birds, mammals, Mesozoic fossils) and illustrates and explains the biology of animals (with well-prepared specimens, etc.).

Tour of the Museum:

Section of a 1,340-year-old North American redwood.

Elephants, including a cast of the Steinheim mammoth, which lived some 200,000 years ago.

Ichthyosaurus skeleton from Holzmaden, about 180 million years old; section of a 13 m (43 ft) long sei whale; other marine mammals.

Animals of Africa, including a nocturnal okapi shot in 1911.

Corals, shellfish, snails, crustaceans.

Beetles, butterflies and moths.

Mesozoic fossils:
sandstone slab with twenty-four eagle-head lizards from Stuttgart-Hedelfingen/Kaltental (about 200 million years old); snake-necked dinosaur from Holzmaden (180 million years old);

Opening times
Tues.–Fri. 10 a.m.–4 p.m.,
Sat. and Sun. 10 a.m.–5 p.m.

Entrance Hall

Central Hall

Courtyard

Dioramas in courtyard

Left Wing

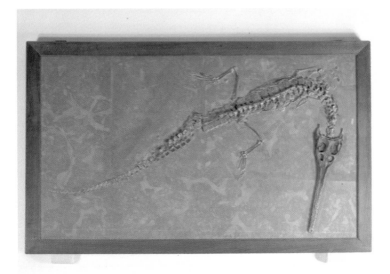

Fossil dinosaur

mammals, with a particularly interesting display of marsupials, including a Tasmanian devil;
primates, including Steinheim Man (about 250,000 years old), found at nearby Steinheim an der Murr in 1933.

Right Wing

Birds (exotic specimens; endangered and extinct species, including the dodo, extinct since 1681, the great auk, extinct since 1844, the North American passenger pigeon, extinct since 1914, and an egg of the Madagascar ostrich, which became extinct in the 17th c.); bird habitat from Iceland.
Local fauna (diorama of small mammals; mammals, birds); species extinct in Württemberg (otter, beaver, lynx, wolf).

New Building

The new building, recently completed, in Nordbahnhofstrasse, on the north-west side of Rosenstein Park, was designed by Siegel, Wonneberg & Partners. It has a display area of some 3,700 sq. m (40,000 sq. ft), together with rooms and workshops for scientists and technicians. The collection is arranged chronologically, beginning with an introduction to the history of the earth and of life. The various periods of geological history are displayed on two floors, with particular emphasis on the Triassic (Bunter, Muschelkalk, Keuper), the Jurassic (Lias, Dogger, Malm), the Tertiary and the Quaternary (particularly the Ice Ages). Among the most notable items are fossil remains of dinosaurs, ammonites, sea-lilies, turtles, giant lizards, fishes, mammoths and giant deer.

The Stiftskirche, with the Old Palace and the Mercury Column ▶

Stiftskirche

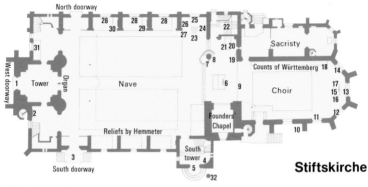

North doorway

1 Tower | Organ | Nave | Sacristy
West doorway
Counts of Württemberg
Choir
Founders' Chapel
Reliefs by Hemmeter
South tower
South doorway

Stiftskirche

1 Stained glass by Stockhausen
2 Tomb of Melchior von Schauenburg
3 Bronze door by Henn
4 Gate Bell (Romanesque)
5 Apostle Doorway
6 Altar Cross
7 "Avenging Angel" by Graevenitz
8 Tomb of J. Brenz
9 Crucifix by Scheible
10 Relief of Christ Crucified
11 Gravestone of Ludwig Fergenhans

12 Stained glass by Kohler
13 Stained glass by Yelin
14 Stained glass by Saile
15 Altar Cross by Henn
16 Golden Pulpit
17 Lectern
18 Praying knight
19 Princely coat of arms
20 The last Minnesinger
21 Tomb of Albrecht von Hohenlohe–Langenburg
22 Tomb of Duchess Johanna Elisabeth

23 Font
24 Christ as sheltering cloak
25 Stained glass by Kohler
26 Late Gothic figures
27 Epitaph of J. Brenz
28 Stained glass by Saile
29 Ulrich von Konstanz
30 Gravestone of H. Heller
31 Tomb of Countess Palatine Elisabeth
32 Bust of Dietrich Bonhoeffer

****Stiftskirche** (Collegiate Church of the Holy Cross)　　　J12(S20)

Location
Stiftstrasse 12

U-Bahn
Schlossplatz

S-Bahn
S 1–6 (Stadtmitte)

Buses
42, 44 (Schlossplatz)

Trams
5, 6, 15 (Schlossplatz)

The Stiftskirche (Protestant), situated in the oldest part of the town, is one of Stuttgart's most familiar landmarks, with its two very dissimilar towers. The oldest part of the church is the lower section of the south tower, which probably dates from about 1175.

The nave was built about 1240. Then in 1320–21 the Beutelsbach Collegiate House, with the tombs of the Counts of Württemberg, was transferred to this site, and Count Eberhard founded the Collegiate House of the Holy Cross. The rebuilding of the choir was completed in 1347. The nave of a Late Gothic hall-church was built by Hänslin and Aberlin Jörg (1495). The south tower was built and then, between 1490 and 1531, the west tower. The church, which became Protestant in 1534, was now in the form in which we see it today.

Only the choir and the towers remained unscathed by the bombing of 1944. Rebuilding was carried out between 1950 and 1959.

Towers

The west tower (61 m (200 ft)) is particularly striking. The massive lower stages are square, with decorated corner buttresses, with a clock on the upper storey, and above these are two octagonal storeys with charming balustraded galleries and a low-pitched tent roof. The blind arcading and the zigzag moulding on the lower part of the older south tower point to Romanesque origins.

Over the Apostle Doorway, the east doorway in the new south wall, are fine figures of Christ and the Apostles salvaged from the old Apostle Doorway which was destroyed during the last war. The modern bronze door (1958) is by J. Weber.
The bronze door of the south-west doorway (also 1958) is by U. Henn; the relief in the tympanum is by Hemmeter. The small Crucifixion group over the choir doorway is 14th c.

Doorway

Notable features of the interior are the tomb of the founders, Count Ulrich and his wife Agnes von Liegnitz (c. 1300), and eleven likenesses of Counts of Württemberg by Sem Schlör (16th c.). Of the old Golden Pulpit there survive the reliefs of the Four Evangelists (c. 1500). Also of interest are the representation of the suffering Christ as a sheltering cloak and the high reliefs of the Annunciation, the Adoration of the Kings and the Circumcision in the Baptistery.
Fine modern works of art are a Crucifix over the choir arch (by M. Scheible, 1943), the stained glass by W. D. Kohler, A. Saile and R. Yelin (1953–54) and the pier supporting the pulpit (by F. von Graevenitz, 1957). The Great Organ was made by the firm of Walcker.

Interior

The largest of the church's bells is the Guilder Bell (the A bell), weighing 104 hundredweight, which was cast in 1520 in Biberach by Martin Kissling, using metal from old cannon. It was rung for funerals, for which a charge of one guilder was made: hence the bell's name. The sound of this bell is said to have inspired Schiller's "Lied von der Glocke" ("Song of the Bell").
The Salve Bell (70 hundredweight) was also cast in the Biberach foundry in the 16th c. According to the astronomer Johannes Kepler it was tolled in the Middle Ages for witch-burnings.
The Gate Bell, now no longer rung because of a crack, is the oldest of the bells, cast in 1285. It was used as an alarm bell.
The small Silver Bell (30 kg (66 lb)) was cast by Pantlion Sidler in Esslingen in 1507. It rings at 9 a.m. and midnight.
In front of the church is a bronze portrait bust (by the Vienna-born sculptor Alfred Hrdlička, 1977) of the theologian Dietrich Bonhoeffer, executed by the Nazis as a Resistance fighter. It was unveiled during an international congress of artists held in Stuttgart in 1977.

Bells

Swabian Centre

See Schwabenzentrum

Swabian Observatory

See Uhlandshöhe

*Tagblatt Tower (Tagblatt-Turm)

K12(T19)

eighteen-storey Tagblatt Tower, 61 m (200 ft) high, was built by E. O. Osswald in 1927–28 as the offices of the

Location
Eberhardstrasse 61

S-Bahn
S 1–6 (Stadtmitte)

U-Bahn
Rotebühlplatz

"Stuttgarter Neues Tagblatt", which ceased publication in 1943. After the Second World War the premises were occupied by the "Stuttgarter Zeitung", which remained here until 1976. Next door to the Tagblatt Tower, at No. 61A, is the municipal cultural centre known as Kultur unterm Turm (Culture under the Tower), opened in 1979. In this building are the Stuttgart Puppet Theatre, the "tri-bühne" (for both see Practical Information, Theatres) and a gallery for special exhibitions (particularly contemporary history and material from the Linden Museum (see entry)).

---

* * Television Tower (Fernsehturm)   M13

Location
Jahnstrasse, Hoher Bopser

Bus
70 (Fernsehturm)

Tram
15 (Ruhbank)

Stuttgart's distinctive landmark, the Television Tower, the first of its kind, rises out of the forest on the Hoher Bopser (see entry), 483 m (1,585 ft) on the southern rim of the Stuttgart Basin, a slender reinforced-concrete needle topped by a four-storey terminal structure and an aerial mast. Its total height, including the aerial, is 216·61 m (711 ft).

This remarkable technical achievement, designed by two engineers, Fritz Leonhardt and Erwin Heinle, with the help of an architect, Rolf Gutbrod, and completed in 1954–56, has provided the model for many similar towers in cities all over the world. The reinforced-concrete shaft, tapering from a diameter of barely 11 m (36 ft) at the base (wall 80 cm (2 ft 7½ in) thick) to 5 m (16 ft) at the top (wall barely 19 cm (7½ in) thick) rests on a base in the shape of a truncated cone, covered with several thousand tons of earth.

Two fast lifts take visitors up to the summit structure in 52·2 seconds. This (renovated in 1982–83) houses on its four floors various operational rooms and a restaurant. From the double viewing platform at a height of 152·40 m (500 ft) there are superb panoramic views. In favourable weather conditions (e.g. before the appoach of areas of low pressure in summer, in situations of temperature inversion in autumn or winter, and sometimes also in foehn conditions) visibility can extend not only to the Black Forest and the Swabian Alb but as far as the Alps.

Town Hall (Rathaus)   J12/13(T19/20)

Location
Marktplatz

U-Bahn
Rathaus

S-Bahn
S 1–6 (Stadtmitte)

Buses
41–44, 84, 85, 87, 92, 93
(Rathaus)

Stuttgart's first Town Hall was a half-timbered building erected in 1456–58 and subsequently much rebuilt and altered; then in 1899 the old building gave place to an imposing new Town Hall designed by Jassoy and Vollmer. A particularly imposing feature was the central tower, 68 m (223 ft) high, in Flemish Gothic style.

On 25–26 July 1944 the Town Hall was destroyed during an air attack, and after the war, in 1953–56, it was replaced by the present building, designed by Schmohl and Stohrer, who incorporated the surviving parts of the old building in the new one. The main block, fronting on to the Marktplatz, is completely new, and has been increased in size by building

Stuttgart's Television Tower, the first of its kind in the world ▶

Town Hall

The Town Hall; in the background the Tagblatt Tower

Trams
1, 2, 4 (Rathaus)

Opening times
Mon.–Fri. 8 a.m.–4 p.m.

Tower and carillon

Façade

Interior

over Eichstrasse. The façade was originally clad with coralline limestone from the Swabian Alb, but this did not prove sufficiently weather-resistant and was replaced in 1976 by a facing of travertine from Gauingen.

The tower of the new Town Hall is 60·50 m (199 ft) high. At the top is a carillon of thirty bells (diameters ranging from 22 cm (8½ in) to 115 cm (3 ft 9 in), weight from 6 kg (13 lb) to 950 kg (2,090 lb)). The carillon, electronically controlled, plays Swabian folk-tunes at 11.06 a.m. and 12.06, 2.36, 6.36 and 9.36 p.m. On the Marktplatz and south-west sides of the tower the phases of the moon and the day of the week are shown beside the normal clock faces.

On the Hirschstrasse front is "Stuttgardia", a bronze figure by Heinz Fritz which was on the tower of the old Town Hall. On the Eichstrasse front is a statue of Hegel by Daniel Stocker, modelled on one by Georg Rheineck.

Ground floor:
Memorial to the fallen (Cannstatt travertine) by J. Brüllmann and W. Schönfeld. By the lift, murals by Walter Wörn, "The Conversation (Work)" and "Wine Festival (Holiday)". On courtyard front, stained glass by Adolf Hoelzel. The bell is from the old Town Hall of 1459.

Upper floor:
Bronze bust (by Dr Fahrner of Freudenstadt) of Theodor Heuss, first President of the Federal Republic and an honorary citizen of Stuttgart. Portraits of Chief Burgomasters from 1862

to 1933. Bust (by Hanne Schorp-Pflumm) of Arnulf Klett, first Chief Burgomaster after the last war.

Reception Room:
"Man of Sorrows" (1510) from the Poor Sinners' Chapel (Arme-Sünder-Kapelle) of the first Town Hall. Stained glass by Wilhelm Saile (designed by Ida Kerkovius). Ludwigsburg porcelain.

Second floor:
Painting by the Abstract artist Willi Baumeister.

Uffkirche

See Bad Canstatt

Uhlandshöhe   H/J14

The Uhlandshöhe, named after the poet and lawyer Ludwig Uhland (see Notable Personalities), is an attractive park, much frequented at week-ends, on the ridge of hills between the city centre and the eastern districts. In the park is a monument to Uhland, with a bust of the poet by Ernst Raus (1965). Lower down the hill is a select residential area.

Bus
42 (Heidehofstrasse)

Tram
15 (Heidehofstrasse)

Visitors to the Swabian Observatory (Schwäbische Stern-warte, Zur Uhlandshöhe 47) after dark can observe the stars and other celestial phenomena (Mon., Wed., Thurs., Fri., Sat. from 8 p.m., Sun. from 2 p.m.; conducted tours).

Swabian Observatory

On the north-western slopes of the hill is the unconventionally designed Waldorf School (an independent school based on the educational principles of Rudolf Steiner). Near by is Rudolf Steiner House, named after the founder of anthroposophy (see Notable Personalities), which houses a variety of cultural and other events.

Waldorf School

*Uhlbach   J/K21

The Uhlbach district (pop. 4,000), still largely rural in character, lies in a sheltered situation in a little side valley on the right bank of the Neckar, above Obertürkheim to the north-east. For more than 750 years wine has been produced here, and the local wine (Uhlbacher) is still much esteemed.

Bus
53 (Uhlbach)

Wine Museum (Weinbaumuseum)   J21

The Stuttgart Wine Museum was opened in the old communal wine-press of Uhlbach in May 1979. It illustrates the history and development of wine production in the Middle Neckar region.
Although the Uhlbach wine-press was built only in 1907, replacing an earlier one which had become too small, it is of some architectural interest, its half-timbered façade and its roof

Location
Uhlbacher Platz 4

Opening times
Apr.–Oct., Sat. 2–6 p.m.,
Sun. 10 a.m.–12 noon and
2–6 p.m.

Tagblath Tower

Outside the Ulbach Wine Museum

Conducted tours
By appointment
(tel. 2 16–28 57)

structure being particularly admired. Features of interest in the museum itself include the massive oak beams of the presses, which were in use until after the First World War; a fully equipped cooper's workshop, with 18th and 19th c. tools; drinking-vessels and wine-containers (of pottery, stoneware, glass and pewter) used over a period of 2,000 years, from Roman times by way of the late Middle Ages to the 19th c.; finely worked wooden casks; and a beautifully carved limewood figure (16th c.) of St Urban, Patron Saint of Vine-growers. The exhibits are well explained and illustrated. The museum includes a wine-tasting room.

In front of the museum is "The Drinker", a half-length figure by Guido Messer.

Untertürkheim G–J17–20

S-Bahn
S 1 (Untertürkheim)

Buses
60, 61

Trams
4,13

Untertürkheim, famed for its excellent wine (Mönchberg and Altenberg vineyards) and as the home of Daimler-Benz, lies on the Neckar above Bad Cannstatt (see entry). The name dates from the Frankish period, when people from central Germany (Thuringia) were resettled here. Viticulture was established in the area as early as the 8th c., and the monasteries of Adelberg, Bebenhausen, Blaubeuren, Denkendorf, Hirsau, Konstanz, Weil and Zwiefalten all owned vineyards in Untertürkheim.

The first railway line in Württemberg, between Cannstatt and Untertürkheim, was opened in 1845. In 1900 the Daimler Motor Company (predecessor of the present-day Daimler-Benz Company) acquired the site in Untertürkheim now

occupied by the Daimler-Benz works, and five years later moved their headquarters here. In 1905 Untertürkheim was incorporated in Stuttgart.
The Württemberg Wine-Growers' Co-operative has large wine-cellars in Untertürkheim.

The church was founded in the 15th c. and altered in the 17th and again at the beginning of the 19th c. During renovation work in 1970 frescoes of about 1660 were discovered. The church contains a notable modern work of art, Grieshaber's "Legend of Joseph".

Protestant parish church

Luginsland is a housing estate developed on garden-city lines by a co-operative association established by Daimler-Benz workers. The first houses were occupied in 1913.
See Daimler-Benz Museum
See Württemberg

Luginsland

Vaihingen

M–S4–8

Stuttgart's Vaihingen ward (pop. 26,000), incorporated in the city in 1942, lies south-west of the city centre on the north-western edge of the Filder Plateau. The place is first mentioned in the records in 1100. Originally belonging to the Counts of Calw, it passed into the hands of the Counts Palatine of Tübingen, who sold it in 1297 to the Esslingen Hospital.
The old village of craftsmen and farmers changed its character when the railway line from Stuttgart to Horb was built. Vaihingen now became an industrial town, and also attracted many new residents from Stuttgart.
Little is left of the older part of the town. Only the Town Hall (built in 1907 by Eisenlohr and Weigle, thoroughly renovated in 1982) remains as an example of local craft traditions.

S-Bahn
Stuttgart-Vaihingen

Buses
81, 82, 84, 86

Trams
1, 3, 14

Stuttgart University has been developing a site at Pfaffenwald since 1964 as a campus for its scientific and technological departments. Among the institutes established here are those concerned with the statics and dynamics of flight and space travel, aero- and gas dynamics, thermodynamics, nuclear energy and plasma research, physics, chemistry, computer studies and building. Features of architectural interest are a small astronomical observatory, the tent roof of the Institute for Light Plane Load-Bearing Structures and an unconventionally designed Students' Pavilion which has attracted much attention.

Pfaffenwald university campus

*Villa Berg

G15

The Villa Berg, on the Höllscher Bühl (Hill) in the Berg district, was built for Crown Prince Karl by Christian Leins (1853). This magnificent and splendidly appointed Renaissance-style country house set in a beautiful park passed after the death of Duchess Vera (1912) to the city of Stuttgart, which used it for receptions and other public occasions. The municipal picture collection was also housed here. After the last war it was taken over by the South German Radio Corporation, which installed

Location
Sickstrasse 1

Trams
4, 9 (Bergfriedhof)

Conducted tours
By appointment

its main studio in the villa, with new radio and television studios in the park.

With its splendid old trees, lawns and fountains, as well as a number of old tombs from the former Berg cemetery, the park became one of the attractions of the 1977 Federal Garden Show. Improvements to the park in preparation for the show included the provision of a link (in the form of a "green corridor" and footbridge) with the Lower Palace Garden.

Villa Reitzenstein   K14

Location
Richard-Wagner-Strasse 15

Tram
15 (Bubenbad)

The Villa Reitzenstein, the official residence of the Prime Minister (Ministerpräsident) of Baden-Württemberg and the offices of the Ministry State, occupies a commanding position on the Gänsheide, to the east of the city centre. This palatial mansion with its domed rotunda was built by Hugo Schlösser and Johann Weirether in 1911–13 for the widow of Freiherr (Baron) Karl von Reitzenstein. During the First World War it was used as a military hospital.

The villa became the property of the *Land* Government in 1924. It was occupied after the Second World War by Dr Reinhold Maier, first Prime Minister of the newly created *Land* of Württemberg-Baden.

Waldau   M/N13/14

Location
Stuttgart-Degerloch

Bus
70 (Königsträssle)

Tram
15 (Ruhbank)

Near the Television Tower (see entry), in the Degerloch district (see entry), is the sports and recreation area of Waldau, Stuttgart's second largest sports complex. It comprises the Waldau District Sports Ground, with a pitch measuring 68 m (78 yd) by 105 m (115 yd), tennis courts covering an area of 60 m (66 yd) by 90 m (98 yd), a 400 m (440 yd) running-track with four lanes and all necessary facilities for field and track events; the Stuttgart University Stadium, with two pitches, a 400 m (440 yd) running-track and two tennis-courts; the Tus Sports Centre, with an indoor swimming-pool, a sports hall, a skating-rink, a curling-rink, a roller-skating rink, a sports kindergarten and bowling-alleys; and eleven club grounds, with fourteen pitches, twenty-three tennis-courts, two indoor tennis-courts, a gymnasium, ten small pitches and facilities for field and track sports.

The Waldau ice-rink has two rinks, each measuring 30 m (33 yd) by 60 m (66 yd). The Waldau District Ground is the home of the Stuttgart Kickers, the local American football team.

Weinsteige   L/M12/13

Alte Weinsteige

Tram
10 (Zahnradbahn)

The Alte Weinsteige, a road which appears in the records as early as the 14th c., runs steeply up from what is now Marktstrasse over the Haigst (a spur of the hills bordering the Stuttgart Basin on the south) to Degerloch. Its name comes not only from the many vineyards in this area but also from its

Villa Berg

Villa Reitzenstein, official residence of the Prime Minister of Baden-Württemberg

function as a route for the wine trade between the Neckar Valley and the upland regions of the Swabian Alb and Upper Swabia. In earlier days the heavily laden drays were hauled up to Degerloch, where there was a changing-station, by teams of anything up to sixteen horses. The maintenance of the road frequently created financial problems for the city and the Ducal Treasury. Pressure on the Alte Weinsteige was relieved by the construction of the Neue Weinsteige and later by the opening of the rack railway (see entry).

Neue Weinsteige

Buses
73–77

Trams
6, 15

In order to reduce the load on the Alte Weinsteige and improve communications between Stuttgart and the Filder Plateau the Neue Weinsteige was built by Eberhard Etzel between 1826 and 1831. From the road, which still runs past vineyards on this sunny slope, there are fine views of the city centre. In the upper part of the Neue Weinsteige is a monument commemorating its constructor.

Weissenburg Park   L13

Location
Ernst-Sieglin-Platz

Buses
73–77

Trams
5, 6 (Bopser)

Weissenburg Park, once the garden of a villa belonging to the industrialist Ernst von Sieglin (1848–1927), combines with the Bopser Park to form a delightful open space affording extensive views. The park was laid out afresh for the 1961 Federal Garden Show, with beautiful flower-beds and lawns and playgrounds for children. The old tea-house (open during the warmer months of the year) is a popular rendezvous.
The park takes its name from the Weissenburg, a castle built in the 13th–14th c. by the Lords of Mühlhausen which was destroyed by the men of Esslingen.
Just outside the park is the Schiller Oak (Schillereiche), now a protected natural feature.

*Weissenhof (Weissenhofsiedlung)   F12/13

Location
Am Weissenhof

Bus
43 (Kunstakademie)

The Weissenhof housing estate (at present in course of renovation), to the east of Killesberg Park, was conceived in 1927 by leading international architects of the day, on the occasion of an exhibition by the German Craft Union (Deutscher Werkbund), as a pattern for the housing of the future. The first plan was prepared by the famous Berlin architect Mies van der Rohe, who formulated his programme in the following words:
"... The problems of housing for our day arise from the changed material, social and intellectual structure of the time; only from this point of view can these problems be understood. The degree of structural change determines the character and the scale of the problems. There is nothing arbitrary about them. They cannot be solved by slogans; nor will slogans make them go away. The problem of rationalisation and standardisation is only part of the problem. Rationalisation and standardisation are merely means: they must never become ends. The problem of housing for our day is basically an intellectual problem, and

Weissenhof: house designed by Hans Scharoun

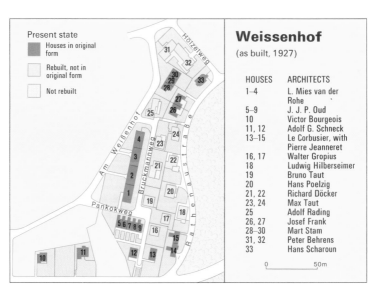

Present state

Houses in original form

Rebuilt, not in original form

Not rebuilt

Weissenhof

(as built, 1927)

HOUSES	ARCHITECTS
1–4	L. Mies van der Rohe
5–9	J. J. P. Oud
10	Victor Bourgeois
11, 12	Adolf G. Schneck
13–15	Le Corbusier, with Pierre Jeanneret
16, 17	Walter Gropius
18	Ludwig Hilberseimer
19	Bruno Taut
20	Hans Poelzig
21, 22	Richard Döcker
23, 24	Max Taut
25	Adolf Rading
26, 27	Josef Frank
28–30	Mart Stam
31, 32	Peter Behrens
33	Hans Scharoun

0   50m

the struggle for new patterns of housing merely an element in the great struggle for new ways of living. . . ."
Mies van der Rohe gathered round him a group of well-known and very individual characters: Walter Gropius from Dessau; Hans Scharoun from Breslau; Richard Döcker from Stuttgart; Peter Behrens, Hans Poelzig, Ludwig Hilberseimer and the brothers Max and Bruno Taut from Berlin; Adolf Schneck from Stuttgart, Adolf Rading from Breslau; Le Corbusier from Paris, J. J. P. Oud and Mart Stam from Rotterdam, Josef Frank from Vienna, Victor Bourgeois from Brussels. Between them they produced a housing estate which was complete and consistent with itself. Unfortunately the Weissenhof estate was damaged during the last war, and the subsequent rebuilding did not follow the original scheme. It is now only the general layout that gives any real impression of the forward-looking ideas of the 1920s.
No. 30 contains a gallery of architecture.

Wilhelma Gardens (Zoological and Botanic Garden)   E/F14/15

Location
Neckartalstrasse

S-Bahn
S 1–3 (Bad Cannstatt)

Buses
52, 55, 56
(Rosensteinbrücke)

The Wilhelma, Germany's only zoological and botanic garden, with magnificent displays of plants and some 8,000 animals from all over the world in more than 1,000 species, is one of the most popular attractions in south-western Germany.
The original nucleus of what have been called "the most beautiful gardens in Europe" was the Wilhelma Theatre at the corner of Pragstrasse and Neckartalstrasse, built for King

Wilhelma Gardens: the water-lily pond and the Nocturnal Animals House

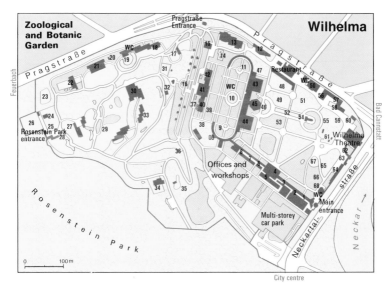

Zoological and Botanic Garden

Wilhelma

City centre

1 Lower Cactus House
2 Tropical birds
3 Tropical House; orchids
4 Winter Garden; Palm House
5 Small Mammals House, Bird House
6 Azalea House
7 Small tropical birds
8 Camellia House
9 Seals
10 Tropical water-lilies
11 Penguins
12 Young Animal House
13 Anthropoid apes
14 Lower apes
15 Spider monkeys, gibbons
16 Subtropical terraces
17 Rock gardens
18 Beasts of prey
19 Lions' Enclosure
20 Big-eared foxes
21 Elephants, rhinoceroses
22 Hippopotamuses, tapirs
23 Ibexes
24 Wild goats

25 Onagers
26 Bisons
27 Oryxes
28 Grévy zebras
29 Communal enclosure
30 Giraffe House
31 Cheetahs
32 Belvedere Café
33 Bongos
34 South American Enclosure
35 Dwarf asses
36 Birds of prey
37 Water-garden
38 Axis deer
39 Upper border
40 Fern Houses
41 Tropical birds, nocturnal animals
42 Useful tropical plants Upper Cactus House
43 Temperature zone aquaria
44 Coral fishes and tropical aquarium
45 Crocodiles, turtles
46 Sea-elephants, sealions

47 Open terraria
48 Playground
49 Wading birds
50 Insectarium; zoo school
51 Riding area
52 Langer See (Long Lake)
53 Wading birds
54 Small beasts of prey
55 Small aviary
56 Old Beasts of Prey House
57 Winter quarters; ring-tailed lemurs
58 Camels
59 Przewalski's horse
60 Black-headed sheep
62 Porcupines, Patagonian cavies
63 Lynxes
64 Brown bears
65 Kangaroos
66 Pheasants
67 Wild pigs, peccaries
68 Kiosk

Wilhelm I in 1839–40 to the design of his Court Architect, L. W. von Zanth (renovation planned). After the completion of the theatre, von Zanth went on to build a "garden-house with residential apartments and ornamental hothouses in Moorish style" (1842–46). The next seven years saw the building of the Banqueting House, the Belvedere, the Picture Gallery and further hothouses and the completion of the garden layout. And in these gardens magnolias, pineapples, camellias,

Tram
14 (Wilhelma)

Boat landing-stage
Wilhelma

Opening times
Daily 8 a.m.–6 p.m.

Conducted tours
By arrangement

rhododendrons, azaleas, orchids and the giant Victoria Regia water-lily still flourish today.

Devastated during the Second World War, the gardens were reconstructed under the direction of the Municipal Gardener, Albert Schöchle.

Animals were gradually introduced into the gardens (e.g. birds and animals featuring in German fairy-tales). The first elephant came to the Wilhelma in 1952. The zoological and botanic gardens proved very popular and were extended in 1963 and subsequently. The year 1967 saw the opening of the Aquarium, which now contains more than 640 species. A year later the houses for pachyderms and beasts of prey, with open enclosures, were opened. The monkey-houses were added in 1975, linking the original Wilhelma Gardens with the new extensions on the borders of Rosenstein Park. In 1977 two new enclosures for South American animals came into use. In 1980 came stabling and enclosures for African ungulates, in 1982 a house for rearing young animals.

The Wilhelma is particularly proud of its successes in breeding animals rarely bred in captivity. In 1965 a sea-elephant was born here; and other animals which have been successfully bred in the Wilhelma include water monitors, king penguins, Siberian tigers, chimpanzees, orang-utans, gorillas, giraffes and Grévy's zebra.

---

*Wilhelmspalais (Municipal Archives)   J13(T21)

Location
Konrad-Adenauer-Strasse 2

U-Bahn
Charlottenplatz

S-Bahn
S 1–6 (Hauptbahnhof)

Buses
42–44, 73–77, 92, 93
(Charlottenplatz)

Trams
1, 2, 4, 5, 6, 15
(Charlottenplatz)

Opening times
Tues.–Fri. 11 a.m.–7 p.m.,
Sat. and Sun. 10 a.m.–4 p.m.

Conducted tours
By arrangement

This Neo-classical palace was built for King Wilhelm I in 1834–40 by the Florentine architect Giovanni Salucci (who was also responsible for the burial chapel on the Württemberg, Rosenstein Palace (see entries) and the Weil manor house at Esslingen (see entry)). The palace was occupied by the princesses Marie (Countess of Neipperg) and Sofie (later Queen of the Netherlands) and later by King Wilhelm II, who abdicated here in 1918.

The palace was badly damaged during the Second World War and was rebuilt in 1961–65 by Wilhelm Tiedje and R. Volz. It now houses the head office of the Municipal Library and the Municipal Archives (which were established only in 1928). In addition to charters and other documents, views of the town and of individual buildings, plans, models and archaeological funds, the collection includes portraits, epitaphs and sculpture. Also of interest are the objects associated with the town's craft guilds (pewter and silver articles, coins and medals). There is an exhibition devoted to the poet Eduard Mörike and his friends (from the collection of Dr Fritz Kauffmann). There are special exhibitions several times a year.

The offices of the Municipal Archives are at Silberburgstrasse 191.

**Württemberg   H20

Location
Stuttgart-Rotenberg

S-Bahn
S 1 (Untertürkheim)

The Württemberg (411 m (1,348 ft)), a hill to the east of the city centre, commands extensive views and once bore the ancestral castle of the Counts of Württemberg; it thus gave its name to the province which now forms part of the *Land* of Baden-Württemberg. The Württemberg family are believed to have

Burial chapel on the Württemberg

come originally from Luxemburg, where the name Widdebirg is recorded as the site of a Sanctuary of the Celtic god Veranus. The chapel of the castle, called Wirtineberc in a document of 1089–90 and Wirtinisberc in a document of 1092, was consecrated by Bishop Adalbero of Worms in 1083. The castle was destroyed by the men of Esslingen in 1311, and after being rebuilt was destroyed by fire in 1519. Thereafter it fell into ruin. The wine-producing village of Rotenberg grew up under the castle walls.

The Württemberg then disappeared from the pages of history until the 19th c., when King Wilhelm I commissioned his Court Architect, Giovanni Salucci, to build a burial chapel on the hill for his wife Katharina, a sister of the Tsar of Russia, who died in 1819. The chapel was built between 1820 and 1824 in the form of a rotunda with four porticoes, probably modelled on the Villa Rotonda at Vicenza. Reliefs of the Four Evangelists were carved for the chapel by the sculptors Dannecker and Thorvaldsen.
In the burial vault are the sarcophagi of Queen Katharina, King Wilhelm I and Princess Marie. The chapel was used from 1825 to 1899 as a Russian Orthodox church.

Bus
61 (Rotenberg)

Opening times
Tues.–Sun. 10 a.m.–noon and 1–5 p.m.

Burial chapel

---

[*]**Württemberg Library** (Württembergische Landesbibliothek)   J13(S21)

The new Württemberg Library, built in 1964–70 to the design of Horst Linde, is a striking modern building with a façade of exposed concrete, copper and clinker brick. It replaced a Neo-Renaissance building of 1883 which was destroyed during the

Location
Konrad-Adenauer-Strasse 8 (entrance in Urbanstrasse)

The new Württemberg Library

U-Bahn
Charlottenplatz

S-Bahn
S 1–6 (Hauptbahnhof)

Buses
41–44, 73–77
(Charlottenplatz)

Trams
1, 2, 4, 5, 6, 15
(Charlottenplatz)

Second World War. It has a main reading-room with seating for 700 readers, storage accommodation for 2·4 million volumes, a large catalogue room and various subsidiary rooms, including a cafeteria. Within the same building is the Library of Contemporary History (Bibliothek für Zeitgeschichte).

Among the library's principal treasures are 7,000 incunabula, 12,500 manuscripts, 12,000 Bibles in more than 100 translations, a Savonarola Collection of the 15th–16th c., a Hölderlin Archive, a First Folio of Shakespeare and the private library of Duke Carl Eugen, the founder of the Württemberg Library.

Behind the Library, in Olgastrasse, is the modern Law Court building (Justizgebäude).

Opening times: Monday to Friday 9 a.m.–8 p.m. and Saturday 9 a.m.–1 p.m.

Württemberg Museum (Württembergisches Landesmuseum) J13(S20)

Location
Old Palace,
Schillerplatz 6

U-Bahn
Schlossplatz

S-Bahn
Stadtmitte

Trams
5, 6, 15 (Schlossplatz)

The Württemberg Museum, founded in 1862, has rich collections of material on the history and culture of Württemberg from the Stone Age to the Jugendstil (Art Nouveau) period and beyond. The museum has been housed in the Old Palace since 1948, but it is only since the restoration in 1971 of the Dürnitz wing that it has been possible to display the collections in accordance with modern principles of museum presentation. The archaeological collection is to be displayed in the Arcade wing of the palace, while the folk collection will be put on show in Waldenbuch Castle, Tübingen. Three floors of the Dürnitz wing and two of the towers are devoted to the

Württemberg Museum, Old Palace

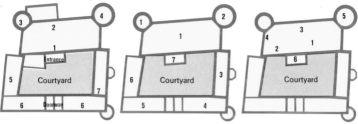

GROUND AND FIRST
FLOORS
1 Textiles and costume
2 Arts and crafts
3 Sculpture
4 Kunstkammer (weapons)
5 Stone Age
6 Bronze and Iron Ages
7 Royal burial vault

SECOND FLOOR
1 Sculpture and altars
2 Kunstkammer (bronzes)
3 Classical Antiquity
4 The Romans in Württemberg
5 The Franks and Alemanni
6 High Middle Ages
7 Staircase (for horses)

THIRD FLOOR
1 Clocks and watches
2 Scientific instruments
3 Musical instruments
4 Coins and gems
5 Kunstkammer (Crown
  Jewels)
6 Staircase (for horses)

museum's main collections; they are linked with one another by the historic old staircase, up which horsemen could ride, as well as by lifts.

The walls are hung with huge tapestries. Costumes and textiles of many different periods and styles are beautifully displayed; they include superb examples of old European lace and ladies' dresses from the mid 18th c. to the 20th c. (e.g. a French silk dress of 1765 and the wedding-dress of the Princess of Hohenlohe-Langenburg, in watered silk with embroidered decoration). Note also the beautiful collection of Baroque sleighs.

An additional floor has been inserted, supported on a structure of light metal. Here visitors can see a representative cross-section of the museum's celebrated collection of applied and decorative art. The carefully selected exhibits, arranged according to style, offer a survey of changing forms from the Middle Ages to the 1920s. Although the museum has the largest collection of Ludwigsburg porcelain, only a few characteristic examples are shown here, since a branch museum devoted to the Courtly art of the Baroque period has been established in Ludwigsburg Palace (see entry).

The main hall on this floor is devoted to sculpture of the medieval and modern periods, reflecting the development of religious art. The central area contains representations of Christ's Passion, while surrounding this are the life of the Virgin, the legends of the saints and the world of angels. The exhibits include numbers of beautiful altars, and in both quantity and quality this is the richest collection of medieval Swabian sculpture. An octagonal case displays liturgical utensils down to the Baroque period. In contrast to the main hall, where the material is arranged according to subject, the sculpture (from the early 13th to the late 18th c.) in the sculpture tower is arranged according to periods and styles, forming a study collection which is both comprehensive and easy to follow.

Opening times
Tues. and Thurs.–Sun.
10 a.m.–5 p.m., Wed.
10 a.m.–7 p.m.
Ground floor

First (mezzanine) floor

Second floor

Iron Age (Hallstatt) jewellery   *Imperial Monument clock*

Other notable items on this floor are stained glass from Alpirsbach (*c.* 1200); eighteen stained-glass panels from Wimpfen am Berg (*c.* 1300); figures of Christ and John from the Lake Constance area (early 14th c.); Mourning Women, from Bronnweiler (1440); Pietà from Weil (1471); Crucifixion from Schwieberdingen (*c.* 1500); Talheim Altar (*c.* 1520); and a drawing on parchment (by J. Syrlin, *c.* 1480) of the tower of Ulm Cathedral.

Third floor

In the main hall are the Coin Cabinet, the Clock Collection and the Collection of Stringed Instruments. The coins are displayed in cases round the walls, arranged chronologically and by countries. There are also some coins in revolving cases, making it possible to see both obverse and reverse sides. The Württemberg coins are displayed separately in an oriel, and in another oriel are gems and cameos. One particularly notable item is a Roman sardonyx cameo (early 3rd c. A.D.) showing Jupiter and Juno enthroned.

In a series of three rooms with a continuous run of wall-cases are sundials and scientific instruments, mainly from the old Kunstkammer. In addition to clocks of the 16th, 17th and 18th c. there is an outstanding collection of beautiful pocket-watches in a separate cabinet. Of special interest is the unique series of seventeen valuable Renaissance watches from the Fremersdorf Collection. Among items of particular local interest are an iron clock of 1530 from the Stiftskirche, clocks made by Johann Sayler of Ulm and the astronomical mechanisms by Matthäus Hahn (1739–98).

Adjoining is the collection of musical instruments, including many locally made keyboard instruments. Two conspicuous items are grand pianos shown at an international exhibition at the turn of the century, with highly decorated cases.

Reached from the third floor is the study room of the textile collection, where embroidery, lace, woven materials, prints, etc., not otherwise displayed can be seen.

Textile study room

The old Kunstkammer of the Dukes and Kings of Württemberg can be seen on four storeys of the south-east tower. The items displayed include weapons, bronzes and a variety of rarities, including the oldest surviving "German" pack of cards (c. 1430). The culmination of the collection is the display of the Crown Jewels of the Kingdom of Württemberg (1806–1918): the crown, sceptre, diadem and necklace (with the twenty-two carat Harlequin diamond), bracelets and ear-rings worn by the queens and a service of gold plate.

Kunstkammer

Prehistory and the early historical period. Stone implements and carvings of the Ice Age hunters. Bronze implements and bronze-casting techniques of the first farmers; gold and bronze jewellery and ornaments from princely tombs at Ludswigsburg, Heuneburg, Hochdorf and Hohmichele. Implements, coins and jewellery of the Celts in the Late Iron Age (4th–1st c.); the Stone Warrior, a life-size sandstone figure (6th c.) from a burial mound at Hirschlanden.

First floor (in course of arrangement)

Vases, bronzes, terracottas, jewellery and glass from Greece and the Greek World and a large collection of Roman Imperial portraits.
The Romans in Württemberg: over 1,000 items displayed in an area of some 250 sq. m (2,700 sq. ft). Sculpture, reliefs and inscriptions on stone, pottery, bronze and iron objects, glass, hoards from the period of Alemannic raids in the 3rd and 4th c. A.D., a silver-plated face helmet from Pfrondorf (Calw district). Early medieval period (3rd–8th c.): one of the richest collections in southern Germany, with fine jewellery and weapons from richly furnished tombs (at Gültlingen, Nieder-stotzingen, Donzdorf, etc.) and the unique wooden objects found at Oberflacht.
High Middle Ages (8th–13th c.): sculpture from Württemberg churches (Hirsau, Unterregenbach, Grosscomburg); bronzes, crucifixes, candelabras, aquamaniles; ivory reliefs (Byzantine casket of c. 100, 10th c. relief of David); goldsmith's work (Ellwangen Casket, c. 870).
Courtly art of the Baroque period: see Ludwigsburg.
In the basement is the Roman Lapidarium (see entry).

Second floor (in course of arrangement)

Württemberg Photographic Archives
(Landesbildstelle Württemberg)

H15

The Württemberg Photographic Archives were established in 1936 as the Stuttgart Municipal Photographic Archives, but their scope was extended in 1936 to take in the whole of Württemberg. This is now a modern audio-visual media centre, with more than 7,000 copies of films, countless slides, photographic portraits, several thousand records and tape recordings and in recent years also video cassettes. With all these resources, and the other facilities it offers, including

Location
Rotenbergstrasse 111

Trams
4, 9 (Bergfriedhof)

Württemberg State Theatres, Great House (interior)

instruction in the use of the various modern media and special exhibitions, the Landesbildstelle attracts many interested inquirers.

*Württemberg State Theatres   J13(R/S21)
(Württembergische Staatstheater)

*Great House (Grosses Haus)   J13(S21)

Location
Oberer Schlossgarten 7

U-Bahn
Staatsgalerie,
Charlottenplatz,
Hauptbahnhof

S-Bahn
S 1–6 (Hauptbahnhof)

Buses
41–44, 73–77, 92, 93
(Charlottenplatz)

Schiller Monument

The Great House of the Württemberg State Theatres was built by Max Littmann in 1909–12. Recently renovated, it ranks among the finest examples of the architecture of the Late Historicist school and has been a scheduled monument since 1924.

This was originally King Wilhelm II's Court Theatre. Here Wieland Wagner produced some twenty operas, and the theatre soon acquired a considerable reputation with its cycles of Wagner's operas and Schiller's plays and its premières of works by Carl Orff. It also became famous as the home of the State Theatre Ballet, to which the choreographer John Cranko and dancers such as Marcia Haydée, Birgit Keil, Edon Madsen and Richard Cragun gained an international reputation.

In front of the Great House is a marble monument to Schiller (by Adolf von Donndorf, 1913). Karl von Donndorf's Destiny Fountain (Schicksalsbrunnen, 1914) commemorates the singer Anna Sutter, who died in 1910, victim of a drama of jealousy.

Little House (Kleines Haus)

J13(R21)

The Little House, a polygonal structure of steel, concrete and glass, was built by Volkart & Partners in 1959–62, replacing the earlier theatre by Max Littmann which was destroyed during the Second World War.

The Little House is the home of the State Theatre (Staatsschauspiel) Company, which in recent years has caused a furore with its interpretations of Brecht and a memorable performance of "Faust" (1977).

In front of the Little House, which harmonises well with its setting in the Palace Gardens (see entry), is "Movement", a piece of sculpture in steel by Bertoni.

Location
Oberer Schlossgarten

Chamber Theatre (Kammertheater)

J13(S21)

The new Chamber Theatre, built in conjunction with the new State Gallery (see entry), was opened in 1983. It is used mainly as an experimental theatre for younger actors and actresses.

Location
Konrad-Adenauer-Strasse

Zoological Garden

See Wilhelma Gardens

Practical Information

It is not always possible to give addresses and/or telephone numbers for all places listed in the Practical Information Section of these guides. This information is readily obtainable from hotel reception desks or from the local tourist office.

Airlines

Most of the major airlines have services to Stuttgart:
British Airways, Kriegsbergstrasse 28, tel. (0711) 29 94 71; at airport 7901 767.
Lufthansa, at airport 7901 467.
Pan Am, at airport 7901 341.
Transworld Airlines, at airport 7901 982/4.

Airport

Stuttgart's Echterdingen Airport, 13 km (8 miles) south-south-west of the city centre, links the city with the international network of air services, with flights to and from many cities in Europe and overseas.

Information
City Air Terminal: corner of Kronenstrasse and Lautenschlager-strasse, tel. 22 12 68. Flight information: tel. 7 90 13 88.

Luggage trolleys
Trolleys (baggage carts) are available for rental.

Airport bus
Route A (not forming part of Stuttgart Transport and Tariff Union) links the airport with Stuttgart Central Station (outside main ticket hall) and City Air Terminal.
Departures from Central Station (City Air Terminal 5–10 minutes later) daily every 30 minutes from 5.25 to 8.55 a.m., every 20 minutes from 8.55 a.m. to 6.55 p.m., every 30 minutes from 6.55 to 10.55 p.m.
Departures from airport daily every 30 minutes from 6.25 to 9.55 a.m., every 20 minutes from 9.55 a.m. to 7.35 p.m., every 30 minutes from 7.35 to 11.35 p.m.

Car parks
Short term car parks, both in the open-air and covered, are available outside the terminal building. Long-stay car parks are situated a short distance away.
A new terminal and an extension to the car park are planned. A new railway station is also to be constructed, with a tunnel leading to the terminal.

Taxis
Taxis can be hired outside the arrivals building. The journey to the city takes about 15 minutes. Tel. 7901 427.

Car rental
The following car rental firms have desks at the airport:
Auto-Hansa, tel. 7901 422; Open: Monday–Friday 7.30 a.m.–10 p.m.; Saturday 8 a.m.–8 p.m.; Sunday 9 a.m.– 9 p.m.
Avis, tel. 7901 451; Open: Monday–Friday 7 a.m.–11 p.m.; Saturday 8 a.m.–9 p.m.; Sunday 9 a.m.–8 p.m.
Europcar, tel. 7901 606; Open: Monday–Friday 7 a.m.–11 p.m.; Saturday and Sunday 8 a.m.–10.30 p.m.

Hertz, tel. 7901 448; Open: Monday–Friday 7 a.m.–11 p.m.;
Saturday 7 a.m.–10 p.m.; Sunday 9 a.m.–11 p.m.
InterRent, tel. 7901 423; Open: Monday–Friday 7 a.m.–11 p.m.;
Saturday 7 a.m.–10 p.m.; Sunday 8 a.m.–10.30 p.m.
Mages, tel. 7901 314; Open: Monday–Friday 7.30 a.m.–
10 p.m.; Saturday 8 a.m.–10.30 p.m.; Sunday 9 a.m.–10 p.m.
Scheer, tel. 7901 614 and 648; Open: Monday–Wednesday
7.30 a.m.–10 p.m.; Thursday and Friday 7.30 a.m.–9 p.m.;
Saturday 8 a.m.–6 p.m.; Sunday 9 a.m.–10 p.m.
Sixt Budget, tel. 7901 504 and 729; Open: Monday–Friday
7.30 a.m.–10.30 p.m. Saturday and Sunday 9 a.m.–8 p.m.

Antiques

Stuttgart has numerous antique shops, often specialising in   Shops
particular (and sometimes unusual) fields or styles. All
categories are represented, from elegant and exclusive
establishments down to junk-shops.

The Baden-Württemberg Association of Art and Antique   Shows
Dealers (Landesverband der Kunst- und Antiquitätenhändler)
holds an annual show of objects for sale. For information about
the date and place of the show enquire of the Stuttgart Trade
Fair and Congress Company (Messe- und Kongress-GmbH),
Am Kochenhof 16, tel. 25 89–1.
Finds can also be made in the large flea-markets in the city
centre in April–May and September and in the summer arts and
crafts market.

Archives

See Libraries and archives

Art galleries

A selection:
Galerie im Hause Behr, Hindenburgbau, Arnulf-Klett-Platz 3,
tel. 28 16 80
Galerie Landesgirokasse, Königstrasse 3, tel. 20 61–1
Galerie Schurr, Alexanderstrasse 153, tel. 60 54 64
Galerie Tilly Haderek, Römerstrasse 1, tel. 60 90 40
Galerie Wahlandt, Olgastrasse 67A, tel. 23 57 57
Inter Art, Hohenheimer Strasse 41
Künstlerhaus Stuttgart, Gutenbergstrasse 62A, tel. 61 76 52
Kunsthaus Bühler, Wagenburgstrasse 4, tel. 24 05 07
Kunsthaus Schaller, Marienstrasse 3, tel. 29 66 46
Kunsthöfle, Überkinger Strasse 15, tel. 53 65 04
Kunststiftung Baden-Württemberg, Gerokstrasse 37
tel. 23 47 20
manus presse, Lieschingstrasse 6, tel. 71 30 37
mueller-roth, Blumenstrasse 15, tel. 24 03 88
Neue Galerie Keim, Marktstrasse 31, tel. 56 56 35
Niedlich, Schmale Strasse 9, tel. 22 32 87
Valentien, Königsbau, tel. 22 16 25
Württembergischer Kunstverein, Kunstgebäude, Schlossplatz,
tel. 29 55 66

Banks

Opening times | Banks and savings banks are generally open from 8.30 a.m. to 4 p.m.; on Thursdays they often stay open until 5.30 p.m. Some close at lunchtime.

Changing money | Money can be changed in all banks and credit institutions during normal opening hours (for extended hours, see below) and in the larger hotels, although here the exchange rate is likely to be less favourable.

Late opening | Deutsche Verkehrs-Kredit-Bank:
Central Station, open weekdays 7.45 a.m. to 9 p.m.; Sundays and public holidays 9 a.m. to 8 p.m.
Airport, open weekdays 7.20 a.m. to 10 p.m.; Sundays and public holidays 8.20 a.m. to 10 p.m.

Landesgirokasse:
Klett-Passage, open Mon.–Fri. 7 a.m. to 7 p.m.

Beer

Stuttgart's beer is famed far beyond the boundaries of Baden-Württemberg. Its four large breweries are Dinkelacker (top brand CD Pils), Sanwald (Weizenbier, light and fizzy), Schwabenbräu (Pilsner and Meisterpils) and Stuttgarter Hofbräu (top brand Herrenpils).
See Restaurants, Beer-houses

Bookshops, Second-hand

Stuttgart is one of the great German centres of book publishing and has many shops selling second-hand books of all kinds.

A selection:
Brockhaus GmbH, Räpplenstrasse 20, tel. 7 80 02 22
Herbert Blank, Traubenbergstrasse 30, tel. 46 30 68
Jürgen Voerster, Relenbergstrasse 20, tel. 29 71 86
Freies Geistesleben, Alexanderstrasse 11, tel. 24 04 13
Margot Lörcher, Wagenburgstrasse 11, tel. 48 11 65
Müller & Gräff, Calwer Strasse 54, tel. 29 41 74
Fritz Neidhardt, Relenbergstrasse 20, tel. 22 33 20
J. F. Steinkopf, Marienstrasse 3, tel. 22 40 21
Stuttgarter Antiquariat, Rathenaustrasse 21, tel. 25 44 21

Book Fair | The Stuttgart Book Fair (Antiquariatsmesse) is held in January in the premises of the Württemberg Art Union (Württembergischer Kunstverein) in Schlossplatz.

Camping and Caravanning

The undermentioned camp site, which is privately owned offers the usual facilities for campers and caravanners. During the summer holiday season reservation is recommended.

Campingplatz Stuttgart-Bad Cannstatt,
Cannstatter Wasen, tel. 56 15 03.
Trams: 1, 2 (Mercedesstrasse)
Bus: 56 (Neckarstadion)
Open throughout the year

Car hire

In addition to the facilities at the airport (see entry) the
following have offices in the town:
Avis, Katharinenstrasse 18
Europcar, Charlottenstrasse 42, tel. 24 773 89
Hertz, Hohenstaufenstrasse 18, tel. 64 30 44

Car parks

(Parkhaus usually means a multi-storey car park; Tiefgarage is
an underground car park.)

DB-Parkhaus, in Central Station
Open 24 hours a day for long-distance travellers

Car parks

Parkhaus Breuninger, Holzstrasse
Open Mon.–Fri. and first Sat. in month 7 a.m.–8 p.m., other
Saturdays 7 a.m.–3.30 p.m.

Tiefgarage Brenninkmeyer, Breite Strasse
Open Mon.–Fri. and first Sat. in month, 7 a.m.–7 p.m., other
Saturdays 7 a.m.–2.30 p.m.

Parkhaus Commerzbank (entrance from Dorotheenstrasse)
Open Mon.–Sat. 7 a.m.–8 p.m.

Tiefgarage Deutsche Bank (entrance Calwer Strasse)
Open Mon.–Sat. 7 a.m.–midnight

Tiefgarage Dresdner Bank, Stauffenbergstrasse
Open Mon.–Fri. 7 a.m.–8 p.m., first Sat. in month 7 a.m.–7 p.m.,
other Saturdays 7 a.m.–4 p.m.

Tiefgarage Landesgirokasse, Marstallstrasse
Open: entrance 6 a.m.–11 p.m., exit 24 hours a day

Parkhaus Hauptbahnhof, Jägerstrasse 17
Open 24 hours a day

Tiefgarage Hertie, Neue Brücke
Open Mon.–Fri. 7.30 a.m.–7 p.m., first Sat. in month 8.30 a.m.–
6 p.m., other Saturdays 8.30 a.m.–2 p.m.

Hofdiener-Garage, Schloss-strasse 25 (corner Schelling-
strasse)
Open Mon.–Fri. 6 a.m.–11 p.m., first Sat. in month 6 a.m.–
7 p.m., other Saturdays 6 a.m.–4 p.m.

Parkhaus Horten-Mitte, Steinstrasse 4
Open Mon.–Fri. 7 a.m.–7 p.m., first Sat. in month 7.30 a.m.–
6 p.m., other Saturdays 7.30 a.m.–2.30 p.m.

Parkhaus Kaufhof, Kronenstrasse
Open Mon.–Fri. 8.30 a.m.–7 p.m., first Sat. in month 8 a.m.–
6.30 p.m., other Saturdays 8 a.m.–2.30 p.m.

Hochgarage Königshof, Stephanstrasse
Open weekdays 7 a.m.–1 a.m., Sun. and pub. hol. 12 noon–
1 a.m.

Kronengarage, Kronenstrasse 20
Open 24 hours a day

Landtags–Tiefgarage, Konrad-Adenauer-Strasse 3
Open weekdays 7 a.m.–7 p.m., Sat. and Sun. day and night

Tiefgarage Landesbibliothek, Konrad-Adenauer-Strasse
Open weekdays 6.30 a.m.–midnight, Sun. and pub. hol. 9 a.m.–
midnight

Liederhalle-Tiefgarage (entrance Breitscheidstrasse)
Open for events in Liederhalle

Marquardt-Garage, Stephanstrasse 33
Open Mon.–Sat. 6 a.m.–1 a.m., Sun. and pub. hol. 11 a.m.–
1 a.m.

Tiefgarage Österreichischer Platz, Tübinger Strasse
Open 24 hours a day

Parkhaus Motorpressehaus, Leuschnerstrasse 1
Open Mon.–Fri. 7 a.m.–7 p.m.

Parkhaus Sophienstrasse, Sophienstrasse 40
Open Mon.–Fri. and first Sat. in month 6 a.m.–8 p.m., other
Saturdays 6 a.m.–4 p.m.

Parkhaus Parkhotel, Neckarstrasse/Kühnstrasse
Open 24 hours a day

Parkhaus Rotebühlplatz, Fritz-Elsas-Strasse
Open Mon.–Fri. 6.30 a.m.–9 p.m., first Sat. in month 6.30 a.m.–
8 p.m., other Saturdays 6.30 a.m.–4.30 p.m.

Rathausgarage, Eichstrasse
Open Mon.–Fri. 6 a.m.–11 p.m., first Sat. in month 7 a.m.–
7 p.m., other Saturdays 7 a.m.–3 p.m.

Schlossgarten-Tiefgarage, Schillerstrasse
Open 24 hours a day

Tiefgarage Kronprinzstrasse, Kronprinzstrasse
Open 24 hours a day

Tiefgarage am Katharinenhospital (entrance Kriegsbergstrasse)
Open Mon.–Sat. 6 a.m.–8 p.m., Sun. 10 a.m.–8 p.m.

Parkhaus Wilhelma, Neckartalstrasse
Open only for visitors to Wilhelma Gardens

Parkhaus Wilhelmsplatz, Bad Cannstatt (entrance Eisenbahn-strasse)
Open Mon.–Fri. and first Sat. in month 8 a.m.–7 p.m., other Saturdays 8 a.m.–3 p.m.

Tiefgarage BW-Bank (entrance by Theodor-Heuss-Strasse and Kienestrasse)
Open weekdays 6 a.m.–11.30 p.m.

Tiefgarage Kronprinzenbau (entrance Kienestrasse/Calwer Strasse)
Open weekdays 6 a.m.–11.30 p.m.

Parkhaus Züblin, Lazarettstrasse 5
Open weekdays 6 a.m.–midnight

Tiefgarage Bohnenviertel, Olgastrasse/Rosenstrasse
Open Mon.–Fri. 7 a.m.–8 p.m., Sat. 7 a.m.–3 p.m., first Sat in month 7 a.m.–8 p.m.

Chemists (Pharmacies)

An after-hours service for the supply of medicines is provided by a rota system under which some shops remain open at night and on Sundays and public holidays. The addresses and telephone numbers of the pharmacists on duty are given in the Stuttgart "Amtsblatt" (Official Gazette) and in the news-papers. All pharmacies display a notice giving the address of the nearest pharmacist on duty. A list of pharmacies can be found in the "Yellow Pages" (die Gelben Zeiten) of the local telephone directory under "Apotheten".

An emergency service for the supply of medicines (Medikamenten-Notdienst) operates at the following times: Saturdays 1.30–10.30 p.m., Sundays and public holidays 8.30 a.m.–10.30 p.m.
Telephone: 22 43 10.

Emergency pharmaceutical service

Concerts

See Music
See Night life

Consulates

Lenzhalde 65, tel. 22 03 59

United Kingdom

Urbanstrasse 7, tel. 24 25 65 and 21 02 21

United States

Cultural institutes

Amerika-Haus,
Friedrichstrasse 23A, tel. 29 23 30

Institut Français,
Diemrshalde 11, tel. 24 59 81

Institut für Auslandsbeziehungen
(Institute for Relations with Other Countries),
Charlottenplatz 17, tel. 22 25–1 47

Italienisches Kulturinstitut,
Kolbstrasse 6, tel. 60 59 80

Kunststiftung Baden-Württemberg
(Baden-Württemberg Art Foundation),
Gerokstrasse 37, tel. 23 47 20

Stuttgarter Künstlerhaus
(Stuttgart Artists' House),
Reuchlinstrasse 4B and Gutenbergstrasse 62A, tel. 61 76 52

Stuttgarter Schriftstellerhaus
(Stuttgart Writers' House),
Kanalstrasse 4, tel. 23 35 54

Currency

The unit of currency is the Deutsche Mark (DM) which is divided into 100 Pfennige.

There are banknotes for DM 5, 10, 50, 100, 500 and 1000 and coins in denominations of 1, 5, 10 and 50 Pfennige and DM 1, 2 and 5.

Exchange rates fluctuate. In May 1987 they were approximately:
£1 = DM 2·9 $1 = DM 1·79
DM 1 = 35p   DM 1 = 55 cents

Customs regulations

Visitors from a country belonging to the European Community may import free of duty the following:
300 cigarettes or 150 cigarillos or 75 cigars or 400 gr tobacco; 4 litres wine and 1½ litres spirits over 22° Gay-Lussac (38·8° proof) or 3 litres fortified or sparkling wine up to 22° proof; 75 gr perfume and 0·375 litre toilet water, together with other goods to the value of DM 500.

If any of the above have been bought in a duty free shop the permitted amounts are approximately one third less; other goods are limited to a value of DM 115. These reduced consessions also apply to visitors from other countries including the United States and Canada.

Disabled, Aid for the

Advice and information can be obtained from the following agencies:

AMSEL (Multiple Sclerosis Society),
Paul-Lincke-Strasse 8, tel. 69 20 19

Behindertenzentrum (Centre for the Disabled),
Heigelinstrasse 13, tel. 7 15 50 97

Caritas,
Olgastrasse 46, tel. 2 10 45–0

Deutsches Rotes Kreuz (German Red Cross),
Nikolausstrasse 6A, tel. 28 08–0
Ambulance Station, Heilmannstrasse 7, tel. 28 08–0

Gehörlosenzentrum (Centre for the Deaf),
Hohenheimer Strasse 5, tel. 24 08 03

Körperbehinderten-Beratungsstelle
(Advice Centre for the Physically Handicapped),
Weimarstrasse 30, tel. 2 16–30 01

Sehbehinderten-Verband Baden-Württemberg
(Society for the Visually Handicapped),
Sonnenbergstrasse 92, tel. 24 14 15

Electricity

The voltage in Germany is 220 50 cycles AC. Visitors from the United States, Canada and Great Britain require a continental adaptor.

Emergency calls

Dial 110 anywhere in the Federal Republic.

Police

See p. 6

Useful telephone numbers

Events

CMT (Camping, Motoring and Tourism Show) on the Killesberg

January

Shrove Tuesday: Carnival parade in city centre

February–March

Great flea-market in city centre

April–May

Spring Festival on Cannstatter Wasen
Swabian Floriade (Württemburg Horticultural Show) in Ludwigsburg

End April–May

Practical Information

May	Stuttgart Horse Fair (with riding tournament)
June	Cannstatt Brezel Festival Anna Scheufele Festival in Stuttgart-Kaltental Craft market in Marktplatz
End June	Fishermen's Festival on Cannstatter Wasen
July–September	Various fairs and festivals in different parts of the city, including the Kannenfest in Cannstatt and the Anna Scheufele Festival in Kaltental
August	Festival of Light on the Killesberg
End August–September	Great flea-market in city centre Wine Village (Weindorf) in Marktplatz, Kirchstrasse and Schillerplatz
September–October	Cannstatt Fair on (See A–Z Cannstadt) Cannstatter Wasen (with the Agricultural Fair every three years)
Second week-end in October	Fellbach Autumn Festival
November–December	Stuttgart Book Weeks in Landesgewerbeamt
December	Christmas Fair in Marktplatz, Kirchenstrasse and Schillerplatz Exhibition of cribs (Nativity scenes) in Old Palace

Events of longer duration

May–October	Summer Theatre, Killesberg Park
May-August	Serenade concerts in courtyard (or in church if weather is bad) of Old Palace
May–September	Concerts on Sunday afternoons and jazz concerts on Sunday evenings in Music Garden of Kurpark, Bad Cannstatt, also cultural events in the afternoon throughout the year

Programmes

Information about the dates and programmes of events can be found in the Stuttgart "Amtsblatt" (Official Gazette), in the monthly "Stuttgarter Monatsspiegel", which is obtainable from the Tourist Office (see Information), ticket agencies (see entry), bookshops and newspaper kiosks, and in the newspapers, which have columns giving information and news about entertainments (e.g. the "Stuttgarter Zeitung's" column "Was? Wann? Wo?").

Excursions

Many travel agencies, bus companies and the German Federal Railways run trips to places of interest in the Neckar Valley, the Swabian Forest, the Swabian Alb and the Black Forest.

The Schwäbischer Albverein (Swabian Mountain Club) has waymarked (signposted) many attractive footpaths in the Stuttgart area. Some pleasant walks can be made from stops or stations on the Stuttgart transport system, following a circular route and returning to the same point.

Excursions by rail: Information
tel. 20 92–54 64.

Excursions on the Stuttgart tram system:
tel. 60 17–1.

City sightseeing tours:
booking and tickets for all city tours (see Sightseeing tours) at the "i-Punkt" tourist centre in the Klett-Passage at the Central Station.

Coach trips:
Verkehrsamt der Stadt Stuttgart, Abteilung 80–6, tel. 22 28–24 1.
Coach tour agencies (e.g. Ruoff, Jäger, Binder, Zauner, Fischle).
Omnibusverkehrsgemeinschaft Bahn/Post (OVG), tel. 20 92–54 64.
Stuttgarter Verkehrsverbund (VVS), tel. 66 06–1.

Neckar cruises: see entry

Sightseeing flights: see entry

Exhibitions

See Museums
See Trade fairs

Food and drink

The cuisine of Swabia, and therefore of Stuttgart, makes use of a good deal of meat and farinaceous food, though vegetables also figure on the menu. The place of potatoes (which are usually eaten baked in their skins, fried or in salad rather than boiled) is often taken by various forms of pasta, in particular the spätzle which are usually made at home and noodles, usually factory-made.

A clear meat soup containing strips of pancake or egg.   Flädlessupp'

Brain soup – regarded as a particular delicacy and mainly served   Hirnsupp'
on special occasions.

A dough of flour, eggs, salt and just a little water to "stretch"   Spätzle
it is the basis of the famous Swabian "spätzle". A good housewife chops the dough into small pieces on her baking board and drops the miniature dumplings into slightly salted boiling water. A more modern way of producing spätzle is to use a sieve-like machine.

147

Practical Information

Leberspatzen
A kind of elongated liver dumpling, eaten either in clear soup or fried, and often accompanied by potato salad.

Maultaschen
These are a particular Swabian speciality – pasta squares filled with minced meat, spinach, and a variety of spices and herbs. They are boiled in meat stock and then served either in the stock or fried in fat, accompanied by potato salad, or alternatively lightly browned with eggs and accompanied by a mixed salad.

Rostbrätle
This is a Swabian beef roast, served with well-fried onions, spätzle and a rich gravy.

Ripple mit Kraut
A substantial dish: rib of pork, boiled and sometimes lightly smoked, accompanied by sauerkraut.

Linsen und Spätzle
Lentils and spätzle, eaten as a quick snack or, accompanied by lightly smoked sausages, as a main-dish.

Romadour und Hefeknapf
Yeast dumplings with Romadour cheese.

Gaisburger Marsch
A Stuttgart "national dish": sliced potatoes and spätzle, often with vegetables (including onions) and a little meat, boiled in meat stock.

Dampfnudeln
Sweet yeast dumplings cooked in milk and sugar.

Hutzelbrot
Hutzelbrot or Schnitzbrot is a kind of sweet bread or cake which is eaten in the weeks before Christmas. It is made from a dark coloured dough with nuts and dried fruit (plums, apples, pears).

Brezel
The brezel (pretzel) is traditionally believed to have been invented in Cannstatt many centuries ago. This brittle savoury biscuit, glazed and salted on the outside, is an almost invariable feature of the Swabian breakfast or afternoon cup of coffee. Buttered brezels are a favourite snack between meals.

Zwiebelkuacha
Zwiebelkuacha (onion tart) is the regular accompaniment to the year's new wine. During the vintage they are sold even in the street markets.

Ochsenmaulsalat
A good Ochsenmaulsalat (ox-cheek salad) is often regarded as the sign of a good butcher. The butchers of the Swabian Mountains are said to prepare the best.

See Beer.

See Wine.

See Restaurants and Cafés.

Getting to Stuttgart

By air
From Great Britain
There are daily direct flights from London Heathrow, operated by British Airways and Lufthansa.

From the United States and Canada
There are good services from the major cities, either direct or via London or Frankfurt.

From Great Britain   By sea and rail
The quickest route from London is via Dover – jetfoil to Ostend – and then by train via Brussels, Cologne and Frankfurt. By leaving London at 8 a.m. passengers arrive in Stuttgart just before 9 p.m. Another route is via Harwich and the Hook of Holland, travelling by the night ferry. This journey takes about 18 hours, but there is the advantage of a night's rest on the ferry.

From the Hook of Holland to Stuttgart the distance is about   By road
410 miles; from Ostend it is about 450 miles, all on motorways.

Hotels

In the Federal Republic of Germany there is no official system of hotel classification, and accordingly the selection of hotels in this list, and the order in which they are listed, is based on general criteria. Luxury hotels are marked with an * asterisk.

The Stuttgart Tourist Office (See information) publishes a list   List of hotels
of hotels in the city. This booklet, "Hotels in Stuttgart", appears annually, giving up-to-date information about the category of the hotel, whether it has a restaurant, the tariff, the number of beds, amenities and services provided and location on a plan of the city. A shorter version of this list is printed in the "Stuttgarter Monatsspiegel" ("The Month in Stuttgart"), which can also be obtained from the Tourist Office or from bookshops and newspaper kiosks.

Rooms can be booked through the Tourist Office (See   Room booking service
Information).

In the following list b.=beds; SP=swimming pool; *=luxury.   Hotels

*Steingenberger-Hotel Graf Zeppelin, Arnulf-Klett-Platz 7,   Central area
400 b. (with *restaurant and grill, Zeppelin-Stüble and Maukanescht wine-bar), SP, sauna, tel. 29 98 81
*Parkhotel, Villastrasse 21, 110 b. (with Radio-Stüble wine-bar), tel. 28 01 61
Am Schlossgarten, Schillerstrasse 23, 169 b. (with Zirbelstude restaurant), tel. 29 99 11
Astoria, Hospitalstrasse 29, 60 b., tel. 29 68 06
Azenberg, Seestrasse 114–116, 76 b., SP, sauna, tel. 22 10 51
Bäckerschmide, Schurwaldstrasse 44, 20 b. (with wine-bar, Intercitywell recommended), tel. 46 60 35
Bellevue, Schurwaldstrasse 45, 21 b., tel. 48 10 10
Berlin, Hasenbergstrasse 49A, 68 b., tel. 62 24 54
Buchenhof, Hasenbergsteige 90, 20 b., tel. 65 20 18
Espenlaub, Charlottenstrasse 27, 40 b., tel. 24 00 22
Geroksruhe, Pischeckstrasse 68–70, 40 b., tel. 24 01 04
Hansa, Silberburgstrasse 114, 100 b., tel. 62 50 83
Haus von Lippe, Rotenwaldstrasse 68, 48 b., tel. 63 15 11
Hotel am Feuersee, Johannesstrasse 2, 54 b., tel. 62 61 01
Intercity-Hotel, Arnulf-Klett-Platz 2, 136 b., tel. 29 98 01

Practical Information

Ketterer, Marienstrasse 3, 100 b., tel. 29 41 51
Kronenhotel, Kronenstrasse 48, 104 b., tel. 29 96 61
Mack, Kriegerstrasse 5–7, 69 b., tel. 29 29 42
Rieker, Friedrichstrasse 3, 80 b., tel. 22 13 11–15
Royal, Sophienstrasse 35, 130 b., tel. 62 50 50
Ruff, Friedhofstrasse 21, 130 b., SP, sauna, tel. 25 01 61
Sautter, Johannesstrasse 28, 80 b., tel. 61 60 33–35
Unger, Kronenstrasse 17, 93 b., tel. 29 40 41
Wartburg-Hospiz, Lange Strasse 49, 100 b., tel. 22 19 91–95
Wörtz, Hohenheimer Strasse 30, 40 b., tel. 24 06 81

Bad Cannstatt	Krehl's Linde, Obere Waiblinger Strasse 113, 32 b., tel. 56 75 67
Spahr, Waiblinger Strasse 63, 93 b., tel. 55 20 08
Sporthotel am Neckarstadion, Mercedesstrasse 83, 46 b.,
tel. 56 52 38
Stoll-Grieshaber, Brunnenstrasse 27, 35 b., tel. 56 23 31
Wiesbadener Hof, Wiesbadener Strasse 23, 33 b.,
tel. 56 12 01–02
Birkach	Haus Birkach, Grüningerstrasse 55, 95 b., tel. 45 00 61
Botnang	Hirsch, Eltinger Strasse 2, 60 b. (popular restaurant),
tel. 69 29 17
Büsnau	*Waldhotel Schatten, Gewand Schatten 2, 66 b.,
tel. 69 10 51–54
Waldgasthaus Glemstal, Mahdentalstrasse 1, 49 b.,
tel. 68 16 18
Degerloch	Waldhotel Degerloch, Guts-Muths-Weg 18, 68 b., tel. 76 17 90
Wielandshöhe, Alte Weinsteige 71–75, 36 b., tel. 64 30 37
Feuerbach	*Europe, Siemensstrasse 26–28, 300 b. (with Granada restaurant), tel. 81 50 91
Striegel (no rest.), Stuttgarter Strasse 58, 35 b., SP,
tel. 81 44 84–85
Heumaden	Seyboldt (no rest.), Fenchelstrasse 11, 24 b., tel. 44 53 54
Möhringen	*Stuttgart International, Plieninger Strasse 100, 300 b. (with Paris Grill restaurant), SP, sauna, tel. 7 20 21
Gloria, Sigmaringer Strasse 59, 130 b., tel. 71 30 59
Neotel-Garni (no rest.), Vaihinger Strasse 151, 120 b.,
tel 7 80 06 35
Panorama-Hotel, Laubweg 1 (Fasanenhof), 23 b., SP,
tel. 7 15 50 15
Anker, Vaihinger Strasse 76, 32 b., tel. 71 30 31
Plieningen	Fissler Post, Schoellstrasse 4–6, 88 b., tel. 45 50 74–76
Traube, Brabandtgasse 2, tel. 45 48 33
Rohr	Sieben Schwaben, Osterbronnstrasse 82, 31 b., tel. 74 43 68
Rotenberg	Rotenberg-Hotel Böhringer, Stettener Strasse 87, 31 b.,
tel. 33 13 43
Stammheim	Novotel, Korntaler Strasse 207, 234 b., tel. 80 10 65
Uhlbach	Krone, Uhlbacher Strasse 225, 15 b., tel. 32 27 35
Münzmay, Rührbrunnenweg 19, 17 b., tel. 32 40 28–29

Alte Krone, Grossglocknerstrasse 4, 30 b., tel. 33 01 05	Untertürkheim
Beisswanger, Augsburger Strasse 331, 46 b., tel. 33 08 93	
Spahr, Klabundeweg 10, 45 b., tel. 33 23 45	
Dachswald, Dachswaldweg 120, 60 b., tel. 68 87 28	Vaihingen
Fremd-Gambrinus, Möhringer Landstrasse 26, 19 b., tel. 73 17 67	
Lamm, Glockenblumenstrasse 1, 62 b., tel. 73 11 74	
Römerhof, Robert-Leicht-Strasse 93, 49 b., tel. 69 10 84	
Vaihinger Hof, Katzenbachstrasse 95, 47 b., tel. 73 19 51	
Aparthotel Wangener Post, Wasenstrasse 15, 64 b., tel. 42 00 81	Wangen
Autohof, Hedelfinger Strasse 17, 48 b., tel. 42 40 81	
Löwen, Ulmer Strasse 333, 60 b., sauna, tel. 42 34 06	
Hirsch, Glemgaustrasse 14, 53 b., tel. 88 32 70	Weilimdorf
Keinath, Spielbergstrasse 24–26, 110 b., tel. 87 53 92	Zuffenhausen
Koetzle, Eschenauer Strasse 27, 71 b., tel. 87 11 37	
°Kongresshotel Schwabenlandhalle, Tainerstrasse 7, 201 b., tel. 0711/5 85 90	Fellbach
Mercure, Siemensstrasse 50, 204 b., tel. 07150/1 31	Korntal-Münchingen
Airport-Hotel Mövenpick, Randstrasse, 160 b., tel. 79 07–0	Airport

---

Information

Lautenschlagerstrasse 3, Postfach 870, 7000 Stuttgart 1, tel. 2 22 80, telex 7 23 854	City Tourist Office
"i-Punkt" (a branch of the Tourist Office), in the Klett-Passage at the Central Station, tel. 2 22 80 Open Mon.–Sat. 8.30 a.m. to 10 p.m., Sundays and public holidays 11 a.m. to 8 p.m. (May–Oct.) or 1–6 p.m. (Nov.–Apr.)	Hotel accommodation and booking
Landesfremdenverkehrsverband Baden-Württemberg, Bussenstrasse 23, tel. 48 10 45–46	Baden-Württemberg Tourist Office
Presse- und Informationsamt der Landeshauptstadt Stuttgart, Town Hall (Rathaus), Postfach 161, tel. 2 16–23 23	City Press and Information Office
See Trade fairs	
See Airport	
See Useful Telephone Numbers	

Libraries and archives

Württembergische Landesbibliothek, Konrad-Adenauer-Strasse 8 (entrance in Urbanstrasse), tel. 2 12–54 24 Trams: 1, 2, 4, 5, 6, 15 (Charlottenplatz)	Württemberg Library

Buses: 41, 42, 43, 44, (Charlottenplatz)
Main reading-room, periodicals reading-room, catalogues and bibliographies are open Mon.–Fri. 9 a.m.–8 p.m., Sat. 9 a.m.–1 p.m.
Newspaper reading-room, special reading-rooms for manuscripts, maps, views, portraits and Hölderlin Archive are open Mon.–Fri. 10 a.m.–1 p.m. and 2–5 p.m.
Music and art reading-rooms are open Mon.–Fri. 10 a.m.–5 p.m., Sat. 9 a.m.–1 p.m.
Library of Contemporary History (books, periodicals, photographic collection and archives covering period since 1914) is open Mon.–Fri. 8 a.m.–5 p.m., Sat. 9 a.m.–noon.

State Archives

Hauptstaatsarchiv, Konrad-Adenauer-Strasse 4, tel. 2 12–53 31
Trams: 1, 2, 4, 5, 6, 15 (Charlottenplatz)
Buses: 41, 42, 43 (Charlottenplatz)
Open: Mon.–Thurs. 9 a.m.–5.15 p.m., Fri. 9 a.m.–3.15 p.m.
Issue of archive material Mon.–Fri. 9–11 a.m. and 1–3.30 p.m.

Municipal Library

Zentrale Stadtbücherei, Wilhelmspalais, Konrad-Adenauer-Strasse 2, tel. 23 34 34
Trams: 1, 2, 4, 5, 6, 15 (Charlottenplatz)
Buses: 41, 42, 43, 44 (Charlottenplatz)
Open: Mon.–Fri. 10 a.m.–7 p.m., Sat. 10 a.m.–1 p.m.
Information on branches and travelling library: tel. 23 34 34

Other institutions

Library of the Institute for Relations with Other Countries, Charlottenplatz 17, tel. 22 25–147
Trams: 1, 2, 4, 5, 6, 15 (Charlottenplatz)
Buses: 41, 42, 43, 44 (Charlottenplatz)
Open: Mon., Wed. and Thurs. 10 a.m.–4p.m., Wed. and Fri. 10 a.m.–9 p.m., Sat. 10 a.m.–noon.

American Library,
Friedrichstrasse 23A, tel. 29 23 30
Trams: 9, 14 (Universität), 5, 6, 15 (Schlossplatz)
Bus: 44 (Schlossplatz)
S-Bahn: Hauptbahnhof
Open: Mon. and Fri. 11 a.m.–6 p.m., Tues. and Thurs. 11 a.m.–7.30 p.m., Wed. 11 a.m.–5.30 p.m.

Library of French Institute,
Diemershalde 11, tel. 24 59 81
Tram: 15 (Eugensplatz)
Bus: 42 (Eugensplatz)
Open: Mon.–Fri. 2.30–6.30 p.m.

Library of Italian Institute,
Kolbstrasse 6, tel. 60 59 80
Trams: 1, 14 (Marienplatz)
Bus: 41 (Marienplatz)
Open: Mon.–Fri. 10 a.m.–noon and 4–7 p.m., Sat. 10 a.m.–noon

South German Library for the Blind,
Siemensstrasse 52, tel. 81 54 51
S-Bahn: S 4–6 (Feuerbach)
Trams: 6, 13 (Maybachstrasse)
Open: Mon.–Fri. 9 a.m.–4 p.m.

Hohenheim University Library,
Garbenstrasse 15, Stuttgart-Hohenheim, tel. 45 01–20 97
Bus: 70 (Hohenheim)
Open: Mon.–Fri. 8 a.m.–9 p.m., Sat. and Sun. 10 a.m.–5 p.m.

Stuttgart University Library,
Holzgartenstrasse 16 (entrance in Max-Kade-Weg),
tel. 20 73–22 22
Buses: 40, 42, 43 (Hegelplatz)
Open: Mon.–Fri. 9 a.m.–7 p.m., Sat. 9 a.m.–4 p.m. during term,
Mon.–Fri. 9 a.m.–6 p.m., Sat. 9 a.m.–noon during vacation

Building Information Centre,
Nobelstrasse 12, Stuttgart-Vaihingen, tel. 66 68–5 00
Bus: 82 (Schranne)
Open: Mon.–Thurs. 9 a.m.–4 p.m., Fri. 9 a.m.–noon

Landesgewerbeamt,
Kanzleistrasse 19/Kienestrasse 18, tel. 20 20–5 57
Tram: 9, 14 (Universität)
Vocational Training Library: Tues., Thurs. and Fri. 10 a.m.–
6 p.m., Wed. 10 a.m.–7 p.m., Sat. 10 a.m.–12.30 p.m.
Industrial documentation and information: Mon.–Fri. 9 a.m.–
3.30 p.m.
Patents and standards: Tues., Thurs. and Fri. 10 a.m.–4 p.m.,
Wed. 10 a.m.–7 p.m., Sat. 10 a.m.–12.30 p.m.
Design Library: Tues.–Thurs. 1–6 p.m.

Lost property offices

Municipal:
Fundbüro der Stadtverwaltung,
Böheimstrasse 8, tel. 2 16–20 16

Railways
Fundstelle der Deutschen Bundesbahn,
Central Station (entrance Cannstatter Strasse),
tel. 20 92–54 68

Post Office:
Fundbüro der Deutschen Bundespost,
Postamt 1, Am Kleinen Schlossplatz,
tel. 2 06 71

Trams:
Fundbüro der Stuttgarter Strassenbahnen,
Filderstrasse 47 (Marienplatz),
tel. 7 88 50

Markets

The principal foodstuff's market is the Market Hall (Markthalle)   Market Hall
in the city centre, where produce from all over the world is
offered for sale.

One of Germany's oldest Christmas markets is held during   Christmas market
Advent in the Marktplatz, Kirchstrasse and Schillerplatz.

Practical Information

Flea-markets

Two large flea-markets are held in the city centre in April–May and September. Because of the numbers of dealers who flock to these markets the dates of the markets are announced only a short time in advance.

Craft market

This is a recently established market, held in the Marktplatz during the summer. The first such market was held in June 1981.

Weekly markets

Marktplatz and Schillerplatz (city centre)
Tues., Thurs. and Sat. 7 a.m.–noon
Feuerseeplatz and Bismarckplatz (Stuttgart West)
Tues., Thurs. and Sat. 7 a.m.–1 p.m.
Marktplatz, Bad Cannstatt
Tues., Thurs. and Sat. 7 a.m.–12.30 p.m.
Rathausplatz, Degerloch
Wed. and Sat. 7 a.m.–noon
Festplatz, Zuffenhausen
Sat. 7 a.m.–1 p.m.
Oberdorfplatz, Möhringen
Sat. 7–11.30 a.m.
Klagenfurter Strasse (in front of Wine-Press), Feuerbach
Sat. 7 a.m.–12.30 p.m.
Bihlplatz, Heslach
Sat. 7 a.m.–noon
Rathausplatz, Vaihingen
Wed. and Sat. 7 a.m.–12.30 p.m.
Ladenzentrum (Shopping Centre), Freiberg
Sat. 7–11.30 a.m.

Griegstrasse pedestrian zone, Botnang
Sat. 7 a.m.–noon

Information about Stuttgart's weekly markets can be obtained from the Market Office (Markamt) in the Market Hall (see entry), tel. 2 16–1

Money-changing

See Banks

Motoring assistance

Information

ADAC (Allgemeiner Deutscher Automobil-Club),
Am Neckartor 2, tel. 28 00–0
ACE (Auto Club Europa),
Schmidener Strasse 233, tel. 5 06 71
AvD (Automobilclub von Deutschland),
Mörikestrasse 30, tel. 77 55 87
DTC (Deutscher Touring Automobil-Club),
Liststrasse 68

Breakdown assistance

ADAC breakdown service (Pannendienst), tel. 1 92 11
ACE breakdown service, tel. 53 44 44
AvD breakdown service, tel. 77 55 18

These will be found in the Yellow Pages telephone directory under the heading "Autoreparatur".

Repair garages

See Radio and television

Traffic information by radio

Museums

For most museums, galleries and collections there is no admission charge.

Admission

Information about current exhibitions is given in the "Stuttgarter Monatsspiegel", published by the Tourist Office (see Information)

Special exhibitions

Albatross Museum of Flight,
Echterdingen Airport, tel. 7 90 16 86
Bus: A (Flughafgen)
Open 9 a.m.–7 p.m.

Museums

Bessarabian Germans, Museum of the
See A to Z

Bible Museum
See A to Z

Catacomb Museum
See A to Z, Esslingen, St Dionysius's Church

City Gallery
See A to Z, Kunstgebäude

Daimler-Benz Museum
See A to Z

Fellbach Municipal Museum
See A to Z, Fellbach, Municipal Museum

Fire Service Museum
See A to Z

German Agricultural Museum
See A to Z

German Playing-Card Museum
See A to Z

Hohenheim:
Collections of Institute of Botany
Collections of Institute of Soil Science and Habitat Study
Economic Archives of Baden-Württemberg
Museum on History of Hohenheim
Zoological and Veterinary Museum
See A to Z, Hohenheim

Kepler Museum,
Am Marktplatz (adjoining Town Hall), 7252 Weil der Stadt
(Life and work of the great astronomer)
S-Bahn: S 6

Practical Information

Open: Mon.–Fri. 9 a.m.–noon and 2–4 p.m., Sat. 10 a.m.–noon and 2–5 p.m., Sun. 11 a.m.–noon and 2–5 p.m.

Ludwigsburg Municipal Museum
(Städtisches Museum),
Kulturzentrum, Wilhelmstrasse 3

Max Nitze Museum of Endoscopy,
Arminstrasse 10

Municipal Archives
See A to Z, Wilhelmspalais

Municipal Lapidarium
See A to Z

National Schiller Museum and German Literary Archives
See A to Z, Marbach

Porsche Museum
See A to Z

Postal History Collection
See A to Z

Roman Lapidarium
See A to Z

State Archives
See A to Z

State Gallery
See A to Z

State Museum of Ethnology
See A to Z, Linden Museum

State Museum of Natural History
See A to Z

Wine Museum
See A to Z, Uhlbach, Wine Museum

Württemberg Museum
See A to Z, Old Palace

Music

Opera and ballet	Württemberg State Theatres, Oberer Schlossgarten 5–7, tel. 20 32–4 44
Concert halls	Liederhalle, Berliner Platz 1
	Musikhalle Ludwigsburg, Am Bahnhof
	Killesberg Halle 4, Am Kochenhof

Festsaal Bethanien,
Onstmettinger Weg 35

Internationale Bachakademie,
Hasenbergstrasse 3

New Palace,
Schlossplatz

St Eberhard's Church,
Königstrasse 7

Gustav Siegle House,
Leonhardsplatz 28

South German Radio Studio,
Neckarstrasse 230

Stiftskirche,
Stiftstrasse 12

Studio of Landesgirokasse,
Königstrasse 5

Waldorf School,
Rudolf-Steiner-Weg 10

For tickets see Ticket Agencies

Neckar cruises

Four boats with bar and restaurant facilities (250–450
passengers) operate on the Neckar from the end of March to
the end of October. They sail from the Wilhelma landing-stage
(dock) in Bad Cannstatt to Marbach (Schiller Museum,
German Literary Archives) and Lauffen, calling at fourteen
other places in this wine producing area.

Short trips to Aldingen and back (advertised in advance):
Sat. 7.30–11.30 p.m. (with dancing)
Tue. 2.30–6.30 p.m. (for senior citizens)
Wed. 6.30–9.30 p.m. (wine cruises)

Trips round the river harbour; daily at 9 and 11 a.m.

Tel. 54 10 73   Information

Newspapers

Stuttgart has two dailies with circulations extending outside
the region, the "Stuttgarter Zeitung" and the "Stuttgarter
Nachrichten", as well as a number of local papers – the
"Canstatter Zeitung", the "Nord-Stuttgarter Rundschau", the
"Untertürkheimer Zeitung" and the "Filderzeitung".

Weekly publications are the "Amtsblatt der Stadt Stuttgart", the city's "Official Gazette" (every Thursday), and the "Stuttgarter Wochenblatt" (Thursday/Friday).

Illustrated periodicals are the Stuttgart edition of the "Regional Magazin" and "Stuttgart Tips".

The national tabloid press is represented by "Bild" (Stuttgart edition).

Subscribers to one of the papers published by the Möhringen Printing and Publishing Centre also receive the Sunday paper "Sonntag Aktuell".

The "Stuttgarter Monatsspiegel" (The Month in Stuttgart), published every month, is the official programme of activities in the city, with information about hotels, theatres, exhibitions, etc.

Night life

Stuttgart, like other large cities, has a range of night-spots and other establishments catering for a variety of tastes. The range extends from beer-houses, with or without unattached ladies and sex films, to high-class night-clubs. The heart of the city's night life is the famous Altstadt (Old Town) around Leonhardsplatz.

See also Restaurants

Night-clubs

Campain, Hirschstrasse 16, tel. 22 59 67 (open until 5 a.m.)
Evergreen, Kronprinzstrasse 6, tel. 29 12 33 (open 9 p.m.–4 a.m.)
Excelsior, Königstrasse 54A, tel. 29 67 73 (open 10 p.m.–5 a.m.)
Four Roses, Leonhardsplatz 24, tel. 24 27 37 (open 10 p.m.–4 a.m.; closed Sun.)
Imperial, Rathauspassage 7, tel. 24 43 28 (open 2 p.m.–5 a.m.; closed Sun.)
Moulin Rouge, Königstrasse 58, tel. 29 47 07

Discothèques

AT-Podium City, Königstrasse 51, tel. 29 48 98 (open 8 p.m.–4 a.m.)
Boa, Tübinger Strasse 12–16, tel. 22 31 13 (open 8 p.m.–2 a.m.)
Coupé, Friedrichstrasse 31, tel. 29 48 49 (open 9 p.m.–4 a.m.)
Monokel, Kronprinzstrasse 30, tel. 29 72 88 (open 9 p.m.–3 a.m.)
Odeon, Fritz-Elsas-Strasse 60, tel. 22 41 70 (open 9 p.m.–2 a.m.)
OZ, Kronprinzstrasse, tel. 29 55 85 (open 8 p.m.–4 a.m.)
Perkins Park, Stresemannstrasse 39, tel. 25 20 62/3 (open Wed.–Sun. 8 p.m.–4 a.m.)
Tanzpalast, Rotebühlplatz 4, tel. 22 44 12 (open 9 p.m.–5 a.m.)
Zorba the Buddha (Bhagwan-Disco), Hauptstätter Strasse 40 (Schwabenzentrum), tel. 23 52 27 (open from 9 p.m.)

AT-Podium City, Königstrasse 51 (from 8 p.m.)
Bruddler, Schloss-strasse 28, (8.30 p.m.–12.30 a.m.)
Cartoon, Graf-Eberhard-Bau, Eberhardstrasse
Dixieland Hall, Ketterer-Keller, Marienstrasse 3 (7.30 p.m.–1 a.m.)
IG Jazz, Fritz-Elsas-Strasse 38

Jazz spots, live music

Kupferschmiede, Christophstrasse 45
Laboratorium, Wagenburgstrasse 147 (from 8.30 p.m.)
˙Maxim, Wilhelmstrasse/Olgastrasse corner
Zum alten Trog, Hauptstätter Strasse 61
Music Garden, Kurpark, Bad Cannstatt (Sun. from 6 p.m.)
Theatrium, Jugendzentrum (Youth Centre), Neckarstrasse 63

Music

Gutshof, Hackstrasse 1B, tel. 26 08 26 (7.30 p.m.–1 a.m.)
Palais, Königstrasse 22, tel. 22 32 52
Rosenau, Rotebühlstrasse 109
Tabaris, Hindenburgbau, Königstrasse 2

Dancing

Europe am Killesberg, Siemensstrasse 26–28, tel. 81 50 91
Treffpunkt-Bar, Flughafen-Hotel, tel. 79 02 11
Intercity-Bar, Central Station, tel. 29 98 01
Parkhotel, Villastrasse 21, tel. 28 01 61
Hotel Royal, Sophienstrasse 35, tel. 62 50 50
Hotel am Schlossgarten, Schillerstrasse, tel. 29 99 11
Steigenberger-Hotel Graf Zeppelin, Arnulf-Klett-Platz, tel. 29 98 81
Hotel Stuttgart International, Plieninger Strasse 100, Möhringen, tel. 7 20 21
Waldhotel Degerloch, Guts-Muths-Weg 18, tel. 76 17 90
Waldhotel Schatten, Am Solitudering, tel. 68 10 51

Hotel bars

Bei Jan (Cafe Künstlerbund), Am Schlossplatz 2, tel. 22 41 49 (until 3 a.m.)
Big Ben, Kriegsbergstrasse 11, tel. 29 73 26 (until 3 a.m.)
Old Ascot, Königstrasse 5, tel. 29 53 33 (until 1 a.m.)
Pianino, Hirschstrasse 36, tel. 29 11 18 (until 2 a.m.)
Rob Roy, Mövenpick, Kleiner Schlossplatz, tel. 22 0034 (until 2 a.m.)
Pantry Pub, Bolzstrasse 6, tel. 29 37 42 (until 2 a.m.)
The Pub, Bolzstasse 7, tel. 22 41 27 (until 5 a.m.)
Tiffany, Schulstrasse 10, tel. 29 26 27 (until 4 a.m.)

Other night-spots

Opening times

The department stores in the city centre and their branches in other parts of the town are open Mon.–Fri. 9 a.m.–6.30 p.m., Sat. 8.30 a.m.–2 p.m. On the first Saturday in the month they stay open until 6 p.m.

Department stores

Individual shops fix their own opening hours. They open between 7 and 9 a.m., frequently close at lunchtime (though not in the central area) and remain open in the evening until 6 or 6.30 p.m.
Some bakers' and butchers' shops, and most hairdressers, close on Mondays.
On the first Saturday in the month ("long Saturday") shops decide individually whether or not to remain open in the

Other shops

afternoon. In the central area they usually do; in the outer districts they usually do not.

Public holidays

Shops are closed on official public holidays (see entry). On Shrove Tuesday most shops close about midday.

Shopping outside normal hours

In the Klett-Passage at the Central Station there are shops selling bread, cakes, pastries and other foodstuffs, books, pharmaceutical and toilet articles, flowers, etc. They open between 6 and 8 a.m. and close between 9 and 10 p.m. (though these out-of-hours shopping facilities may be discontinued).

For the days and hours when banks, car parks, libraries and archives, museums, post offices, restaurants and spa establishments are open, see the appropriate entries.

Opera

See Music

Postal services

Important post offices

Head Post Office (Hauptpostamt, Postamt 1),
Bolzstrasse/Kleiner Schlossplatz
Open: Mon.–Fri. 8 a.m.–6 p.m., Sat. 8.30 a.m.–12.30 p.m.

Postamt 102,
Central Station, tel. 29 03 56
Open: Mon.–Sat. 6 a.m.–11 p.m., Sun. 7 a.m.–10 p.m.

Postamt 23,
Airport, tel. 79 50 55
Open: Mon.–Fri. 8 a.m.–noon and 2–5.30 p.m., Sat. 8 a.m.–noon.

Poste restante
(Postlagernd)

Mail addressed poste restante can be sent to either the Head Post Office or the post office in the Central Station.

Public holidays

The following public holidays (on which shops are closed) are observed in Stuttgart:
New Year's Day (1 January); Shrove Tuesday (afternoon); Good Friday, Easter Day and Easter Monday; 1 May; Ascension Day; Whit Sunday and Whit Monday; Corpus Christi; German Unity Day (17 June); Day of Prayer and Repentance; Christmas Eve (24 December, afternoon); Christmas Day and 26 December; New Year's Eve (31 December, afternoon).

Public transport

VVS

Stuttgart's S-Bahn (suburban railway), buses and trams have combined to form the city's Transport and Tariff Union

(Verkehrs- und Tarifverbund Stuttgart, VVS), so that the same tickets are used in all these forms of transport.

Verkehrs- und Tarifverbund Stuttgart, Rotebühlstrasse 133, tel. 66 06–1

Information

The VVS tariff system, complicated in itself, depends on self-service and may thus pose problems for the visitor. If you expect to make several journeys of some length in the course of a day, the best plan is to buy a twenty-four-hour ticket, which is easy to use. Calculating the fare according to the zonal tariff is more difficult. The fare depends on the number of zones traversed in the course of a journey.

Tariff system

VVS tickets are valid on the S-Bahn (suburban railway system), on Federal Railways trains (not subject to a supplement on the fare) running on S-Bahn lines and on the Stuttgart–Böblingen, Marbach–Backnang and Kornwestheim–Untertürkheim lines, on trams and buses (except the airport bus, route A) of the Stuttgart transport system and on certain mail bus routes. For details consult the VVS tariff and timetables, available at all stations and principal bus and tram stops.

Validity of tickets

Single tickets are valid for a single journey (which may involve a change of vehicle). They do not require to be cancelled.

Single tickets

Children under six travel free; children between six and twelve pay according to the children's tariff.

Children

Multiple tickets have five sections, each valid for a single journey in the central area. The sections may be used either for several journeys by the same person or for the same journey by more than one person. The sections must be validated by cancellation in a cancelling machine.
The A type of multiple ticket is valid within one zone in the central area.
The B type is valid for all zones in the central area.
The K type, for children, is valid in all zones in the central area.

Multiple tickets

Twenty-four-hour tickets are obtainable either for the central area only or for the whole VVS network.

Twenty-four-hour tickets

Congress tickets (minimum of twenty with same starting date; children half price) are issued for those attending congresses, conferences and similar events; they are valid for either two, three or four days.

Congress tickets

A two-city ticket, valid for twenty-for hours, allows the holder to use tram, bus and rail services in any two of the following transport areas: Berlin, Bonn, Bremen, Cologne, Frankfurt, Hamburg, Hannover, Mannheim/Ludwigshaften, Munich, Nürnberg/Fürth, Rhine/Ruhr, Stuttgart.
These tickets can be bought at the larger railway stations and at official travel agencies.

Two-city tickets

The "jumbo ticket" (Jumbo-Karte) and "Sunday saver" (Sonntags-Sparkarte) offer reductions for families.

Special offers

Hand baggage, prams, wheel chairs, etc., are carried without charge.

Hand baggage

Practical Information

U-Bahn (Underground)

Stuttgart has no Underground in the normal sense, though some tram (street car) routes run underground. The stops are marked by a white U on a blue background.

Stadtbahn

The tramway company (SSB) is at present developing part of its system into a new Stadtbahn (city railway). Prototypes of the new vehicles are already in experimental operation in Stuttgart.

Radio and television

Radio and television programmes in the Stuttgart area come from the South German Radio Corporation (see A to Z), the studios and offices of which are housed in a modern tower block complex in Neckarstrasse and in the Villa Berg.
Two of South German Radio's channels, SDR I and III, broadcast traffic information.
The Second German Television Service (ZDF), South-West Radio (SWF) and the American Forces Network (AFN) also have studios and transmitters in Stuttgart.

Rail travel (trains)

Information

General travel information (trains, railway buses) is available in the main hall of the Central Station: tel. 29 97 11

Express goods – despatch: tel. 20 92–54 28
Express goods – collection: tel. 29 20 30
Fares information: tel. 20 92–1
House-to-house luggage delivery: tel. 20 92–54 47
Motorail: tel. 20 92 54 64
Railway bus excursions: tel. 20 92–55 40
S-Bahn – train information: tel. 20 92–1
Seat reservation: tel. 20 92–54 15
Special trains: tel. 20 92–54 64

Timetable information

Services to Munich, Austria and the Balkans: tel. 1 15 31/32
Services to Nürnberg, Hof, Berlin, the German Democratic Republic and Czechoslovakia: tel. 1 15 33
Services to Friedrichshafen, Lindau and the Allgäu: tel. 1 15 34
Services to Konstanz, Switzerland and Italy: tel. 1 15 35
Services to Karlsruhe, France and Basle: tel. 1 15 36
Services to Frankfurt am Main and Wiesbaden: tel. 1 15 37
Services to northern Germany and the Benelux countries: tel. 1 15 38

Railway station

Stuttgart's Central Station (see A to Z) is a major centre of domestic and international passenger train traffic, and is also the point of intersection of all the city's S-Bahn routes, many tram routes and numerous local, regional and long-distance bus routes. From here long distance trains depart in all

directions, and Stuttgart is served by German Federal Railways'
inter-city network.

Facilities available at the station: left luggage office, luggage
lockers, post office, Intercity Hotel, restaurants, Railway
Mission, exchange office, luggage despatch office, shops
(provisions, books and papers, souvenirs), cinema.

Restaurants, wine bars, beer houses and cafés

See Hotels Restaurants in hotels

Times, where given, denote the latest hour at which hot meals
are served; days given are those on which a restaurant is closed.
Exceptionally high-class restaurants are marked with an
asterisk.

°Alte Kanzlei, Schillerplatz 5A, tel. 29 44 57 (until 11.45 p.m.) Central area
°Alte Post, Friedrichstrasse 43, tel. 29 30 79 (Sun. and pub.
hol.)
°Brunner (vegetarian), Hauptstätter Strasse 40, tel. 24 06 60
(Sun.)
°China Garden, Königstrasse 17, tel. 22 38 68
°Mövenpick Rôtisserie Baron de la Mouette (Swiss), Kleiner
Schlossplatz, tel. 22 00 34 (until midnight)
°Martin's Stuben, Karl-Schurz-Strasse 15, tel. 26 16 31
°Scheffelstuben, Haussmannstrasse 5, tel. 23 40 42 (Sat. and
Sun.)
Aldar (Egyptian), Marktstrasse 6, tel. 24 50 03
Alter Simpl, Hohenheimer Strasse 64, tel. 24 08 21 (until
midnight)
Bopserwirt, Neue Weinsteige 8, tel. 6 40 71 43
Börse, Heustrasse 1, tel. 29 26 98 (Sat. and Sun.)
China-Koch (Chinese), Holzstrasse 23, tel. 24 48 55
China Town (Chinese), Eberhardstrasse 6, tel. 24 72 71
Churrasco (Argentinian), Hirschstrasse 14, tel. 22 35 67
Come Prima (Italian), Steinstrasse 3, tel. 24 34 22 (Sun.)
Eden (self-service), Eberhardstrasse 1, tel. 58 14 36 (until
10 p.m.)
Goldener Adler, Böheimstrasse 38, tel. 64 17 62 (Mon.)
Greiner-Stuben, Hindenburgbau, Arnulf-Klett-Platz 1,
tel. 29 51 21 (until 11.30 p.m.)
Korfu (Greek), Olgastrasse 51B, tel. 23 46 14
Kupferschmiede, Christophstrasse 45, tel. 23 35 30
Marché (self-service), Königstrasse 16 (until 10 p.m.)
Maredo (Argentinian), Friedrichstrasse 35, tel. 29 66 74
Mira (Yugoslav), Calwer Strasse 46, tel. 29 36 30 (until
1.30 a.m.)
Poseidon (Greek), Reinsburgstrasse 13, tel. 61 81 39 (until
midnight)
Ratskeller, Marktplatz 1, tel. 24 49 51 (until midnight)
Schwyzer Eck (Swiss), Neckarstrasse 246, tel. 26 58 90
(Mon.)

Alt Cannstatt, Königsplatz 2, tel. 56 11 15 (until 11.30 p.m.; Bad Cannstatt
Mon.) Filderhof, Remschneiderstrasse 12, tel. 54 45 19 (Mon.)

Rössle, Eltinger Strasse 41, tel. 69 21 30 (Sun. and Tues.) Botnang

Practical Information

Degerloch	*Fässle (French), Löwenstrasse 51, tel. 76 01 00 (Sat.) Goldener Bär, Löffelstrasse 24, tel. 76 58 76 (Mon.) Amazonas (Brazilian), Auf dem Haigst 46, tel. 76 23 80 (Tues.) Fernsehturm (restaurant and grillroom in Television Tower), Jahnstrasse 120, tel. 24 61 04/05 (until 11 p.m.)
Feuerbach	*Lamm, Mühlstrasse 24, tel. 85 35 16 (Sun. and pub. hol.)
Gablenberg	Hasen, Gablenberger Hauptstrasse 91, tel. 46 47 00 (Sat.) St Petersburg (Russian), Gablenberger Hauptstrasse 20
Heslach	Waldheim Heslach, Dachswaldweg
Mühlhausen	*Öxle's Löwen, Veitstrasse 2, tel. 53 22 26 (Sun. and pub. hol.)
Plieningen	Nagelschmiede, Brabandtgasse 1, tel. 45 74 54 (Tues.) Traube, Brabandtgasse 2, tel. 45 48 33 (Sat. and Sun.)
Riedenberg	Stiftsstuben, in Augustinum, Florentiner Strasse 20, tel. 47 58 04
Untertürkheim	Eisernes Kreuz, Grossglocknerstrasse 20, tel. 33 02 89 Maharadja (Indian), Inselstrasse 147, tel. 33 18 78 (until midnight; Mon.)

Cafés

Of Stuttgart's many cafés the following are currently the most popular:

In city centre	Schweickhardt im Marquardt, Königstrass 22 Königsbau, Königstrasse 28 Nast, Neue Brücke 3 Sommer, Charlottenplatz 17 Stöckle, Johannesstrasse 76
Bad Cannstatt	Kripp, Bahnhofstrasse 1 Schwarz, Augsburger Strasse 356

Wine-bars

Central area	Arche, Bärenstrasse 2, tel. 24 57 59 (Sun. and pub. hol.) Cottastüble, Cottastrasse 4, tel. 6 49 12 76 Kachelofen, Töpferstrasse 6, tel. 24 23 78 Radiostüble, Villastrasse 21, tel. 28 01 61 (until midnight; Sun. and pub. hol.) Schellenturm, Weberstrasse 72, tel. 23 48 88 (Sun.) Steidle, Böblinger Strasse 161, tel. 6 40 51 57 (Wed. and Sun.) Stuttgarter Stäffele, Buschlestrasse 2A, tel. 61 72 76 (until 1 a.m.; Sun.) Träuble, Gablenberger Hauptstrasse 66, tel. 46 54 28 (until midnight; Sun.) Trollinger, Rotebühlstrasse 50, tel. 62 14 41 (Sun.) Viertelestonner, Hirschstrasse 36, tel. 29 11 18 Zur Kiste, Kanalstrasse 8, tel. 24 40 02 (Sun.) Zur Kochenbas, Immenhofer Strasse 33, tel. 60 27 04 (Thurs.) Zur Weinsteige, Hohenheimer Strasse 30, tel. 24 06 81 (Sat. and Sun.)

* Bäcka-Metzger, Aachener Strasse 20, tel. 54 41 08 (Sun. and Mon.)   Bad Cannstatt
* Zaiss, Erbsenbrunnengasse 5, tel. 56 38 27 (Thurs. and Sun.)
Jägerhof, Hallschlag 145, tel. 54 43 04 (Fri. and Sat.)
Pfund, Waiblinger Strasse 61A, tel. 56 36 69 (Sat.)
Schreinerei, Zaissgasse 4, tel. 56 74 28 (Sun. and pub. hol.)
Urban, Haldenstrasse 44, tel. 54 47 75 (Mon.)

* Hirsche, Maierstrasse 3, tel. 71 13 75 (Sun.)   Möhringen

Paule, Augsburger Strasse 643, tel. 32 14 71 (Thurs. and last   Obertürkheim
Sun. in month)

* Hasen, Innsbrucker Strasse 5, tel. 32 20 70 (Sun. and Mon.)   Uhlbach
Krone, Uhlbacher Strasse 225, tel. 32 27 35 (Mon.)

Haufler, Pforzheimer Strasse 268, tel. 88 22 50 (Wed.)   Weilimdorf

See Wine   "Besenwirtschaften"

Beer-houses

Alt Berlin, Calwer Strasse 48, tel. 22 37 47 (until 2 a.m.; Sun.)   Central area
Bierakademie, Olgastrasse 86, tel. 24 20 27 (until 3 a.m.)
Bierdorf (formerly Königshof), Königstrasse 18, tel. 29 08 55
Bierhaus West, Seidenstrasse 41, tel. 29 59 17
Cockpit, Lautenschlagerstrasse 20, tel. 29 70 03

Holz-Klotz, Wildunger Strasse 41, tel. 56 00 03 (Sun.)   Bad Cannstatt
Männeken Pis, Brunnenstrasse 12, tel. 56 15 81 (Sun. and pub. hol.)
Quellenstüble, Nürnberger Strasse 172, tel. 52 12 72 (Tues.)
Zunftstüble, Schmidener Strasse 102, tel. 55 26 49 (Sun.)

See also Beer, Food and Drink

Shopping

Stuttgart's many high-class shops, often with very un-
pretentious exteriors, have given the city a high reputation as a
shopping centre. The principal shopping streets and
squares are Königstrasse, Calwer Strasse (with the Calwer
Passage), Marienstrasse, Kronprinzenstrasse, Hirschstrasse,
Schulstrasse, Kirchstrasse, Stiftsstrasse, Marktplatz, Kleiner
Schlossplatz and Arnulf-Klett-Platz (with the Klett-Passage).

Shops worth particular attention:

Bleyle-Sauer, Neue Brücke 1
Fine jerseys, fashion knitwear, underwear

Holy's, Königstrasse 54A
Men's fashion (mainly Italian), from young avant-garde to
classic styles

Beate Mössinger, Calwer Passage
Exclusive women's fashion and accessories

Bally, Königstrasse 21
High-class designer shoes

Breuninger, Marktplatz
A department store on the British or American model with a
wide range of goods

Bührle's Pfeifenarchiv, Calwer Passage
Pipes and tobacco goods

Sightseeing flights

Flights from Stuttgart-Echterdingen Airport:
Filderfluggesellschaft, tel. 7 90 16 05 or 79 22 79
Rall Air Luft-Taxi, tel. 7 90 18 43 or 69 88 89

Sightseeing tours

Historical walks

From April to October, every Saturday morning, there are
guided walks, alternately devoted to "Bürgerliches Stuttgart"
(the Stuttgart of the burghers) and "Fürstliches Stuttgart" (the
Stuttgart of the Dukes). The walks start from the courtyard of
the Old Palace at 10 a.m.

Round-Stuttgart trail

The "Rössleweg" is a 53 km (33 mile) circuit on the hills
around the Stuttgart Basin, through forest, orchards and
vineyards. It can be taken in easy stages, with access to public
transport at many points. It is signposted with the black
Stuttgart horse in a yellow circle. An illustrated map is available
from the "i-Punkt" tourist information office (see Information).

City coach tours

"Beautiful Stuttgart" ("Das schöne Stuttgart"): a tour of the
city, starting from the Hindenburgbau (opposite the Central
Station):
1–30 April, daily 2–4 p.m., Sundays also 10 a.m.–noon
1 May–30 September, daily 10 a.m.–noon and 2–5 p.m.
1–31 October, daily 2–4 p.m., Sundays also 10 a.m.–noon
1 November–31 March, Sat. 2–4 p.m., Sunday 10 a.m.–noon

"New Stuttgart" ("Das neue Stuttgart"): modern develop-
ments (four routes):
Beginning of April to end of October, Saturdays 2.15–5.30 p.m.
Departure from Hindenburgbau

"Stuttgart Nights" ("Stuttgarter Nächte"): Stuttgart's night
life, with visits to five night-spots:
Throughout the year, Wed., Thurs. and Fri. 7.30 p.m.–1.30 a.m.
Departure from Hindenburgbau

Spas

Mineral-Heilbad Cannstatt,
at Kursaal, tel. 2 16–46 70 and 2 16–45 36.
Tram: 2 (Kursaal).
Indoor pool with warm, naturally carbonated water (heated to

about 29 °C (84 °F) on Mon., Wed., Fri. and Sat., 26 °C (79 °F) at other times).
Open Mon. 6.30 a.m.–5.15 p.m., Tues.–Fri. 6.30 a.m.–6.45 p.m., Sat. 6.30 a.m.–3 p.m., Sun. 7–11 a.m.
Treatment establishment, with medicinal baths (naturally carbonated chalybeate water, water containing natural calcium chloride), massage, Russian/Roman steam baths, mud packs, light baths, inhalations, Kneipp treatment, the "Stuttgart treatment".
Open Mon.–Fri. 6 a.m.–7 p.m., Sat. 6 a.m.–12.30 p.m.

Mineralbad Berg,
Am Schwanenplatz 9, tel. 26 10 60.
Trams: 1, 2, 14 (Mineralbäder).
Indoor and outdoor pools.
Open Mon.–Fri. 6 a.m.–8 p.m., Sat. 6 a.m.–7 p.m., Sun. 6 a.m.–8 p.m. (indoor pool only 6 a.m.–1 p.m.); admission only up to one hour before closing time.
Medicinal bath with naturally carbonated chalybeate water, heated; massage and under-water massage.
Open Mon.–Fri. 7 a.m.–8 p.m., Sat 7 a.m.–1 p.m.; admission only up to one hour before closing time.
Thermal exercise bath:
Open Mon.–Sat. 8 a.m.–7 p.m., Sun. 8 a.m.–noon; admission only up to one hour before closing time.

Mineralbad Leuze,
Am Leuzebad 2–6, tel. 28 32 24 and 28 32 27.
Trams: 1, 2, 14 (Mineralbäder).
Indoor and outdoor pools with naturally carbonated water.
Open: pool daily 6 a.m.–9 p.m., treatment establishment Mon.–Fri. 6 a.m.–7.30 p.m., Sat. 6 a.m.–1.30 p.m., Sun closed.

Mineralbad Breuninger,
Marktstrasse, tel. 21 98-7 90.
Trams: 1, 2, 4, 5, 6, 15 (Charlottenplatz).
Buses: 41–44 (Charlottenplatz).
Water temperature 28–30 °C (82–86 °F); sauna, massage.
Open Mon.–Sat. 6 a.m.–9 p.m., Sun. 8 a.m.–4 p.m.

Heilbad Hoheneck
See Ludwigsburg.

Sports

Sportamt der Stadt Stuttgart,
Hirschstrasse 22, tel. 2 16–32 78

Information

Sportkreis Stuttgart,
Neue Brücke 6, tel. 22 30 23

See A to Z, Cannstatter Wasen.
See A to Z, Hanns Martin Schleyer Hall.
See A to Z, Neckar Stadium.
See A to Z, Waldau.

Sports centres

Waldebene Ost (Waldebene Stuttgart-Ost recreation area).
Waldsportpfad für Ältere (for older people; at the Waldheim Raichberg in the Waldebene recreation area).

Nature trails in woodland (Waldsportpfade)

Kräherwald (Stuttgart-West; near Kräherwald District Sports Ground, MTV-Platz).
Waldau (Stuttgart-Degerloch; near Waldau District Sports Ground).
Föhrich (Stuttgart-Feuerbach; adjoining Wilhelm Braun Sports Park).
Steinprügel (Stuttgart-Hedelfingen; at SKG Hedelfingen ground).
Weidachwald (Stuttgart-Hoffeld; Hohe Eiche sports area).
Katzenbachsee (Stuttgart-Büsnau; near Max Planck Institute car parks).
Fasanengarten (Stuttgart-Weilimdorf; near SG Weilimdorf and TSV Weilimdorf grounds).
Schlotwiese (Stuttgart-Zuffenhausen; Schlotwiese District Sports Ground).
Withau (in the Withau Forest west of Stuttgart-Stammheim).
Vita-Parcours (near the Kappelberg, in Fellbach).

Golf

Mönsheim golf-course (between Leonberg and Pforzheim).

Swimming pools

Indoor pools

Leo-Vetter-Bad,
Landhausstrasse 192

Stadtbad Cannstatt,
Hofener Strasse 17

Stadtbad Feuerbach,
Wiener Strasse 53

Stadtbad Heslach,
Mörikestrasse 62

Stadtbad Plieningen,
Im Wolfer 40

Stadtbad Sonnenberg,
Kremmlerstrasse 1

Stadtbad Untertürkheim,
Inselstrasse 145

Stadtbad Vaihingen,
Rosentalstrasse 15

Stadtbad Zuffenhausen,
Haldenrainstrasse 31

Alfred-Reichle-Bad (Bad Cannstatt),
Krefelder Strasse 24

Höhenschwimmbad Hannibal,
Im Asemwald 54

Römerbad im SI (Möhringen),
Plieninger Strasse 100

tus-Schwimmbad (Degerloch),
Königsträssle 37

Hallenbad Fasanenhof,
Laubeweg 1

Freibad Möhringen,
Hechinger Strasse 112

Outdoor pools

Freibad Rosental (Vaihingen),
Rosentalstrasse 21

Freibad Sillenbuch,
Trossinger Strasse 1

Höhenfreibad Killesberg,
Beim Höhenfreibad 37

Inselbad Untertürkheim,
Inselbad 4

ASV-Freibad (Botnang),
Furtwänglerstrasse 122

MTV-Freibad (Botnang)
Furtwänglerstrasse 147

Freibad Schlotwiese (Zuffenhausen),
Hirschsprungallee 12

Freibad Fellbach,
Untertürkheimer Strasse

Taxis

To call a taxi from anywhere in the city dial 56 60 61.

Telephone

The telephone code for Stuttgart is 0711. This prefix must be
used when dialling outside the city limits. Within the city no
prefix is required.

To Great Britain 0044
To the United States and Canada 01
From Great Britain to Stuttgart 01049711
From the United States and Canada to Stuttgart 01149711

International Calls Dialling
Codes

Television

See Radio and television

Theatres

Tickets can be obtained from the "Tourist Zentrum i-Punkt",
from ticket agencies (see entry), by phone direct from the
theatre or through reception desks of principal hotels.

Practical Information

Theatres

Stuttgart

Württembergisches Staatstheater (Württemberg State Theatre), Oberer Schlossgarten 6, tel. 20 32–44 4
Grosses Haus (Great House: opera, ballet, operettas)
Kleines Haus (Little House: drama and ballet)
Kammertheater (Chamber Theatre)
Foyer of Little House (experimental drama, rehearsals)

Altes Schauspielhaus (Old Theatre),
Kleine Königstrasse 9, tel. 22 55 05
Reserve theatre; visiting companies

Theater der Altstadt,
Charlottenplatz, tel. 24 43 42
Literary and experimental drama, youth theatre

Renitenz-Theater,
Königstrasse 17, tel. 29 70 75
Literary drama, cabaret, children's theatre (Kruscheltunnel) in Landesgirokasse Studio

Komödie im Marquardt,
Bolzstrasse 4, tel. 29 14 84
Light theatre

Theaterhaus Stuttgart,
Wangener Strasse 241
Contemporary theatre, musical theatre

tri-bühne,
Kultur unterm Turm, Eberhardstrasse 61A, tel. 23 46 10

Variété-Theater Killesberg,
Höhenpark Killesberg, tel. 25 11 97
May–October

Theater im Westen,
Rotebühlstrasse 89, on the Feuersee, tel. 62 31 54
Modern theatre

Scherbentheater, Künstlerhaus,
Reuchlinstrasse 4B
Contemporary theatre

Dreigroschentheater am Bopser,
Etzelstrasse 9, tel. 60 60 00

studio theater stuttgart,
Hohenheimer Strasse 44, tel. 24 60 93
An amateur company with a wide repertoire

Theater in Augustinum,
Altenstift Augustinum, Florentiner Strasse 20,
Stuttgart-Riedenberg

's Theaterle der Käsreiter,
Gasthof Sonnenberg, Rembrandtstrasse 190,
Stuttgart-Sonnenberg

Theater des Menschen im Forum 3,
Gymnasiumstrasse 21, tel. 29 71 74

Irrlicht-Theater,
Augustenstrasse 14/1, tel. 64 18 03

Makal-City-Theater,
Marienstrasse 12, 4th floor (City-Passage), tel. 62 62 08

Stuttgarter Studentenbühne,
Breitscheidstrasse 3, tel. 65 13 12

Stuttgarter Volkstheater,
in Rebstöckle, Böblinger Strasse 105, tel. 24 62 80

Novalis-Bühne,
Ostendstrasse 106

Schauspielhaus,   Esslingen
Strohgasse 1, tel. 35 67 97
Home of the Württembergische Landesbühne Esslingen

Studio am Blarerplatz

Schwabenlandhalle   Fellbach
Visiting companies

Kongresshalle   Böblingen
Visiting companies

Cabarets

Renitenz-Theater, Königstrasse 17, tel. 29 70 75   Stuttgart
Laboratorium, Wagenburgstrasse 147
Spectrum, Neckarstrasse 67
Theatrium, Jugendzentrum (Youth Centre), Neckarstrasse 63
Les Lee, Kronprinzbau, Calwer Strasse

Brett'l im Klosterkeller, Calwer Strasse 25, tel. 22 07 42
Cafe Merlin, Furtbachstrasse 14, tel. 6 49 16 89
Tante Rosa, Schloss-strasse 28, tel. 29 65 15

Vier-Peh-Podium, Flandernstrasse 99   Esslingen
Galgenstricke, Obstkeller, Webergasse 9

Theater im Keller, Marktplatz 12   Ludwigsburg

Puppet theatres

Stuttgarter Puppen- und Figurentheater,
Kultur unterm Turm, Eberhardstrasse 61A, tel. 29 51 59

La Plapper Plap,
Jugendhaus Ost, Gerokstrasse 7, tel. 24 18 49

Theater am Faden,
Böblinger Strasse 139, tel. 60 48 50

Kruscheltunnel: Renitenz-Theater

Ticket agencies

"i-Punkt", tel. 22 28–0
Klett-Passage, at Central Station
Theatres, concerts, sporting and other events

Kartenhäusle,
Kleiner Schlossplatz, tel. 29 55 83
Theatres, concerts, sporting and other events; Komödie im Marquardt, Theater der Altstadt, Renitenz-Theater, Stuttgarter Puppentheater

Kartenlädle in offices of "Filder-Zeitung",
Vaihinger Markt 20, Stuttgart-Vaihingen, tel. 73 30 21
Komödie im Marquardt, Theater der Altstadt, Renitenz-Theater

Musikhaus Mayer,
Bad Cannstatt, tel. 56 17 30

Südwestdeutsche Konzertdirektion,
Charlottenplatz 17, tel. 20 03 49

Württembergische Staatstheater,
Theaterkasse (Box Office), tel. 20 32–4 44

Komödie im Marquardt,
Theaterkasse, tel. 28 14 84

Renitenz-Theater,
Theaterkasse, tel. 29 70 75

Theater im Augustinum,
Theaterkasse, tel. 47 02–80 35

Time

Germany observes Central European Time (Mitteleuropaische Zeit). This is one hour ahead of Greenwich Mean Time, six hours ahead of New York Time. Sunner Time (Daylight Saving Time) in Germany is two hours ahead of Greenwich Mean Time.

Tipping

In hotels and restaurants a service charge is almost invariably included in the bill. It is usual, however – if satisfied with the service given – either to round up the amount of the bill or to give a specific gratuity. Taxi drivers, usherettes in theatres and cinemas (movie theatres), cloakroom attendants (hat-check girls) and lavatory attendants normally expect a small tip.

Trade fairs

Information

Information about all trade fairs and exhibitions in Stuttgart can be obtained from the Stuttgart Trade Fair and Congress Company: Stuttgarter Messe- und Kongress-GmbH, Am Kochenhof 16, tel. 25 89–1

Annual events

Stuttgart Antiques Fair (in Kunstgebäude)	January
CMT (Caravanning, Motoring and Tourism Show)	End January
Motor Show	End April
ISA (International Collectors' Exchange) SÜDBACK (Bakery and Confectionery Fair)	May/June
HAFA (Consumer Goods Fair)	Spring
HOBBY ELEKTRONIK (Practical Electronics and Micro-computer Show)	September/October
District Medical Association Congress on Further Education VKA (Show of Baden-Württemberg Association of Art and Antique Dealers)	November

In alternate (even-numbered) years

INTHERM (International Fair, "Energy+Technology")	March
INTERGASTRA (International Fair of the Hotel, Restaurant and Confectionery Trades)	April
AMB (Metal-Processing Fair)	September/October

In alternate (odd-numbered) years

GARTEN (Gardeners' and Flower-Lovers' Show)	March
FENSTERBAU (Window Manufacturers' Fair)	June
SICHERHEIT (International Security Fair) FAREGA/FATRAMA (International Combine Show)	Autumn
"das moderne büro" ("The Modern Office")	September/October
ELTEFA (Electrical Engineering and Electronics Fair)	October

At longer intervals

R (International Shutter and Sun-Protection Show)	Spring
INTERVITIS (International Wine-Making Show), with German Wine-Makers' Congress	May
OPTICA (International Optical Fair)	May
Exhibition of Energy Saving and Warmth Retention	September
INTERBAD (International Baths and Balneology Show) Agricultural Fair	September/October

Travel Agents

Any reputable travel agent will book travel to and accommodation in Stuttgart. Information can be obtained from:
British Association of Travel Agents, 53 Newman Street, London W.1.

American Society of Travel Agents, 4400 MacArthur Boulevard, Washington, DC 2007.

Wine

Stuttgart, the "city amid forests and vineyards", is one of Germany's largest wine-producing communes. The best vineyards are those on the sunny side of the Stuttgart Basin and the slopes of the Schurwald.

Most of the area under vines is used for growing red-wine grapes, in particular the Trollinger vine. In recent years wines made from Müller-Thurgau, Riesling, Silvaner and Kerner vines are not so popular as they were formerly.

Among local wines particularly esteemed are Cannstatter Halde, Cannstatter Zuckerle, Obertürkheimer Kirchberg, Obertürkheimer Schlossberg, Stuttgarter Mönchhalde, Stuttgarter Weinsteige, Uhlbacher Götzenberg, Uhlbacher Steingrube, Untertürkheimer Diethof, Untertürkheimer Mönchsberg, Fellbacher Lämmler and Fellbacher Rotberg.

"Wine trails"
(Weinlehrpfade)

A "Weinlehrpfad" can be described as an educational walk through the vineyards and wine producing establishments, the object of which is to give the participants some idea of the work and processes involved in the production of wine. Explanatory signs along the route inform the walker about the methods used in the cultivation of vines. Once again, the Tourist Information Office will provide full details.

Uhlbach–Rotenberg
Begins and ends at Old Wine-Press (Alte Kelter) in Stuttgart-Uhlbach; length 3·2 km (2 miles)
S-Bahn: S 1 (Obertürkheim)
Bus: 63 (Uhlbach)

Zuffenhausen–Max-Eyth-See
Begins Kelterplatz, Zuffenhausen, ends Max-Eyth-See; length 6 km (3¾ miles).
Tram: 15 (Kelterplatz Zuffenhausen)
Bus: 52 (Kelterplatz Zuffenhausen)
Fellbach Wine Trail on Kappelberg
Bus: 60 (Untertürkheimer Strasse)

Wine Cruises

See Neckar cruises

"Besenwirtschaften"

After Christmas and New Year, when business in the wine trade is less brisk and casks must be got ready for the new vintage, some wine-producers open their wine-shops for a few days or weeks, depending on how much wine they have to sell, and announce the fact by displaying a broom (*besen*) of twigs and straw outside the door. These establishments are known as "Besewirtschaften" ("broom inns"), or in Swabian dialect "bäsawirtschäftla".

The following is a selection of "Besenwirtschaften":

Bad Cannstatt

Wilhelm Bauer, Auf der Steig 33, tel. 54 58 55
Melanie Schweikhardt, Pragstrasse 48, tel. 54 49 51

Degerloch

Gustav Gauder, Meistersingerstrasse 23, tel. 76 28 10
Karl Gohl, Epplestrasse 54, tel. 7 65 46 99